DEFECTOR:

A TRUE STORY OF TYRANNY, LIBERTY AND PURPOSE

By Mark Hobafcovich with Paul Dragu

ENDORSEMENTS

Defector is a riveting story of heroism, redemption and finding freedom against all odds. Hobafcovich's harrowing journey from Communist Romania to present-day America will captivate your attention and lift your spirit by turns. This book is a refreshing read about God's grace that will leave readers inspired to follow the stirrings of their own hearts."

—Jonathan Merritt, author of *Jesus is Better Than You Imagined*; Senior columnist for Religion News Service

"Once in a while you will notice the zeal and tenacity of a particular leader that is uncommonly high compared to 'the norm.' Mark is one of those leaders. In reading his story, you begin to understand the genesis of his rare and dogged resolve. Mark has indeed lived life on 'the other side of the fence.' His words are sure to inspire a flagging faith and an absent gratitude for those of us long mired in the unfortunate mediocrity of 'the norm.' A highly recommended read."

—Jeff Christopherson, Toronto-based Author of *Kingdom Matrix: Designing a Church for the Kingdom of God*; North American Mission Board Vice President for Canada and Northeast U.S.

"Who doesn't love to read a tragic story with a triumphant ending? Better yet, to read a true story that blesses and builds you all at the same time. Read and grow!"

—**Johhny M. Hunt,** Senior Pastor of First Baptist Church Woodstock, in Woodstock, Georgia; Author and Former President of the Southern Baptist Convention.

"I do believe that we need this book to be published. It is a true story of a young man, who faced multiple hardships, who overcame and reveals the power of a transformed life."

—**Frank S. Page,** Author, President and Chief Executive Officer of the Southern Baptist Convention Executive Committee

"It's true. Mark Hobafcovich lived *in tyranny a*nd he journeyed from tyranny to purpose − both literally and spiritually! The literal fence was Romania. But, the spiritual fence was monomania! The literal journey was from Romania to Australia to the U.S.A. But, the spiritual journey was from Self-Focus to Jesus Follower to Disciple-maker! His story, life and this book, culminates in Jesus' last words − 'Go make disciples!' How would I know? I know because Mark's been helping me get to the other side of the fence spiritually. Discipleship that is Life-on-Life, Heart-to-Heart and Idea-into-Action. And this book can do the same for you. Buy it. Read it. Apply it."

—**Daniel Grissom,** Chief Executive Officer, Ph.D. in Results

*How does someone go from an obscure
village in a closed communist country to traveling the
world proclaiming the ultimate message of liberty?*

CONTENTS

DEDICATION

MARK:

To the best daughters a father could ask for, Hadassah and Elizabeth, who inspired me to put pen to paper, or more accurately, words to screen. And to my wonderful wife, Christine—thank you for your support and 30 years of selfless love, your encouragement and dedication to the work of the Kingdom, and for never complaining but always assuring. I love you all!

PAUL:

To the fathers, brothers, and uncles who've risked their lives for freedom. And to my parents, who left everything they knew to give us a shot.

AUTHOR'S NOTE

To write this book, I relied on my memory and collaborated with those people portrayed in this account with whom I am still in contact. I am especially grateful to my wonderful wife for the many detailed recollections she has stirred up. For their protection, I have changed the names of most, but not all, of the individuals in this book. The following events are accurate with no composite scenes or characters. The events that seem most incredulous were specifically targeted for factual scrutiny, as to refrain from diminishing their significance. In many cases, dialogue has been cleaned up, or adapted for the sake of flow and exposition. But the spirit of all dialogue remains true to each character and situation.

PROLOGUE

Imprisonment. Forced labor. Permanent separation from family. Maybe even death.

I knew what happened to people who were caught attempting to defect. But I was young and wasn't going to be deterred. When you're young, you don't believe the bad possibilities apply to you. They're for everyone else.

I thought of the rewards. I would live in the West. I would work and make money. I would do what I wanted, *when* I wanted. What more could an ambitious young man ask for?

Once Genu came running to me, I was more concerned with implementing his escape plan than with the fact that I was now harboring a fugitive. He knew the way, he had the plan, and now he had little choice but to try again. He was finished in the motherland.

Genu's impending doom would be the catalyst for my long-awaited escape.

We devised a plan, revised it, and ultimately, carried it out.

What happened over the coming years was nothing like I envisioned. This is my story.

PART I

-1-
THE BORDER

The watchtowers stood yards away. The possibility of a new life and the bridge to a different world, one without tyranny, was within sight. We needed one last good push.

We hadn't slept, eaten or drank since the day before. There was some ham and cognac when we started out, but we didn't ration it so well. We still had cigarettes left. Any comfort was welcomed. At that point, I would have gladly traded my pack of Snagovs for a warm fire – I'd been cold ever since our defection two days before. I was fantasizing about my parent's wood-burning stove back in Bozovici and could almost feel the warmth just thinking about it.

The frozen and sleet-drizzled Romanian soil soaked through my wool gloves and left me with little choice but to take them off. I envied the guys who wore the leather ones. Since it was just two days before Christmas of 1980, I suppose I should've been glad the weather wasn't worse. A few years before, we were hit with such a mighty blizzard that I couldn't leave my apartment for a week.

We lay on our backs, tilted our heads forward, and supported our shoulders with our elbows, waiting for the darkness to settle and provide cover. Our immediate aim was simply to be quiet and stay out of sight of the armed border soldiers. The landscape ahead was vast and wide open. Aside from a few pathetic scattered bushes here and there, and a number of large hay bales up ahead, there was little to hide behind. If there was any upside, it was that we'd passed the cemetery, where I managed to slip my foot into a poorly dug grave.

Genu, about seven years older than my 20 and the first of my friends to bravely attempt defection over a month ago, was on my left. Nick, Johnny and Lucian were huddled together 20 yards behind us. They were a misfit bunch: Nick was almost 30 and serious; Johnny was younger and serious about eluding his troubles; and Lucian was barely old enough to understand what he'd gotten himself into. They would whisper-holler to us every few minutes, asking if we "see anything." We usually responded by patting the air down, urging them to keep quiet.

Once it was fully dark and some time had passed, I turned and asked, "Genu, how long are we waiting here?"

Something was wrong. His eyes were frozen wide open and the muscles on his right jaw twitched as if a heart were beating below the surface. I had seen that look before, when we were lost yesterday.

I tried again a minute later. "Do you think there's anyone watching us?"

"Yeah…I do," he answered, pursing his lips. "Do you see them?" He kept his eyes fixated ahead.

I slowly scanned around as if my head were a periscope. "No. Where?" I finally asked.

He inhaled deeply through his nose.

"If they see us, what do you think they'll do?" I asked.

He explained that the official protocol for border soldiers was to yell out, "Stop or we'll shoot!" But many had been killed by giving escapees a forewarning. "So now they skip the formalities and just start shooting."

"So, you don't see them?" he asked incredulously.

I squinted, hoping to make up for what I was missing.

"Look over there!" he said, shooting his index finger straight. "Right by that hay bale! Do you see the rifle hanging off his back?"

I looked again. In front of the hay bale, I saw the silhouette of a man holding what undoubtedly was the AK-47-like rifle Romanians knew all soldiers to possess. It was pointing to the sky.

"Yeah…yeah. I see him," I said, nodding my head. I only saw him for a second, before he paced back to the other side of the hay bale. But that was enough to send my heart into a furious rhythm and trigger a frightening chill all over my body.

While we waited for what seemed like eternity, I was startled by a rustling sound. It came from one of the sickly bushes just feet away. What appeared to be a fox lazily strolled out from behind the bush. I had seen a fox or two in my life. I once found a closed trap with nothing but the remains of a leg in its grip. It appeared to have belonged to a fox. What's more, it looked to have been chewed off – probably by its owner – above the grip of the trap's metal teeth. I heard this about foxes; they'll mutilate themselves if their freedom is at stake.

This was one peculiar fox. Although it noticed us, it was not spooked. Maybe the lack of rest and nutrition was getting to me, but it appeared this fox knew we were in no position to pose a threat. Before moving on, it came closer. It stared at us for a few seconds, almost mocking us.

I hadn't seen anyone else since the dark figure with the big gun had paced back in front of the hay bale. The only sound was that of the howling wind and our grumbling stomachs. We can't sit in this cold field forever, I thought. I opened my mouth to say something, but stopped. Genu was trembling. His eyes looked blank, as if no one was home. God only knew what sinister memories ran through his mind. I never was convinced he had told me everything about his time as a border soldier.

"They're here," he said. "They're going to get us," he whispered.

"Where?" I nervously asked. The wind seemed to have quieted down just so I could listen intently.

The guys in the back were getting impatient. "What are we waiting for?" Nick whispered. "Let's go!"

If we were going to escape, we had to move. We couldn't wait any longer. We agreed that going back was not an option, not only because of our determination, but because of the possible consequences. Anyone caught anywhere in the border zone without a special pass was to be treated like a defector. The best-case scenario if you were captured was that you'd get worked to the bone on the Danube Canal, a punishment, which did not omit the chance of death by any means. I wondered where Florin and Boots were now, the two other guys who were with us until yesterday.

I started to slowly bring my body up.

"What are you doing?" Genu asked.

"I'm going," I told him.

"No! Stay down and keep quiet! Do you want to be shot?"

"Genu, we can't stay here forever!" I said.

My only close encounter with death to that point was barely escaping the grip of a violent, rushing river when I was 12.

As I slowly brought my torso up, I expected to hear an exploding rifle and feel the sensation of a bullet ripping through flesh. Genu did too, as his expression of horror increased with every inch he watched me rise closer to the sky. I couldn't let his fear infect and paralyze me. It was now or never.

Once I was halfway up, I began walking crouched over. I became more courageous with every step I took. I picked up speed and crept along without looking back. I pushed all thoughts of doubt and fear aside and focused on point B.

I slammed my back against a bale of hay and took a deep breath. Then I slowly sidestepped around it until I got to the edge of the other side. I crouched down and inched my left eye past the edge. A howling wind ripped through and almost pushed me over. As I struggled to keep my balance, I realized there was no one else there. No dark figure. No big gun. No sign of anyone. I stood up straight and waved the guys over.

We'd been watching the guards and making notes since yesterday. But we still had a problem. Even though we were closer, it was still too dark to see. We could barely make out the watchtowers, much less where the guards in or around them stood.

"What do you guys think?" Lucian asked. We were lined up, knees to chest, back resting on the hay bale.

"Guys, look!" Nick said, pointing. "They look bigger from here."

The turf ahead was littered with the remains of large trenches. They spanned about 10 feet wide. Time, weather, and maybe human hands, had done a poor job of filling the holes with dirt and water. Further on the horizon, right on the tip of sight, Johnny noticed a congregation of lights.

"That's probably a Yugoslav village," Genu cut in.

"That's it. Let's go toward it," I said.

As we inched toward the trenches, we heard a whistling unlike that of the wind. In the direction of the sound we saw a flashlight pointing up. The bright light, in combination with the overall darkness, made it difficult to see the holder of the flashlight. We were warned we might run into something like this. We detoured as far right as we could. Lucian started to say something, but Nick put his hand over his mouth.

We heard the trenches were dug for national security reasons. What was now left of them swallowed us up to our waists. My denim jeans did not take the cold mud well. It was hard work crossing through the heavy, semi-frozen, wet muck. I don't know if we ever hit bottom, but I don't think we did. Fortunately, we only had to cross three or four trenches.

We were now very close to the towers. And yet, there was still no sign of any soldiers. There was also no fence connecting the towers like we expected. I couldn't decide if I should be worried or relieved.

I realized I had gotten a little ahead of everyone. My friends were lagging. Some of them were wiping mud off their pants and one looking for a lost shoe. I wanted to keep moving, but decided to wait.

We huddled together. "Where are they?" Nick asked. We looked at Genu. He shrugged his shoulders.

"I say we run," Johnny said.

No one wanted to go first. Nick started to, but Lucian's reluctance stopped him. So I took the lead.

We were running just fine until Lucian, who was still lingering, started coughing. The sound reverberated over the open landscape as if magnified by a megaphone. If there was anyone within earshot, I couldn't imagine them not hearing the coughing. We all shushed Lucian until we were all shushed out. Johnny reminded the young Lucian what awaited all of us if he didn't stop coughing. He tried to stop coughing. He really did. He covered his mouth, he put his head down. He didn't know what else to do. Nothing seemed to help. Even the threat of flesh-tearing bullets and backbreaking forced labor made little impact. The boy was going to cough and there was no stopping him.

I thought for sure we were done. "Dear God," I said under my breath. "Don't let us get caught like this." I was envisioning the sad letters I would be writing to my parents, describing the harsh climate, the hunger in my stomach, and the inhumane treatment at the hands of the heartless brigade leaders of the labor camps.

But just as suddenly as the coughing started, so it stopped. He was done. It was out of his system. We were still alive and, more importantly, seemingly undetected.

We ran past the watchtowers as fast as our heavy legs would allow. I didn't look up or to either side. I had no idea if anyone was there. I didn't want to know. If anyone was there, they must've been asleep.

The open field ahead lay flat and lifeless. Not much different from what we'd seen so far, except for one minor detail: it was all white. The whiteness was not attributed to a recent snow cloud. It was like mud. It was wet and it stuck to your shoes. But it was also like paint because the texture was slippery and smelled like some kind of synthetic chemical. I guessed it may have been a kind of sealant used on homes. Why there was a field of it, I still have no idea. Just like there was no time to ruminate on the whereabouts of the watchtower soldiers, there was even less for identifying the crazy pasty mud, which was now joining the conventional mud on my shoes and jeans.

I was running. In my haste, I almost forgot about my friends. I reassured myself that they were big boys and continued running.

We eventually crossed the white field. My body had warmed a bit, a much needed respite from the cold.

As visible as the clutter of lights beyond were becoming, they were no match for the natural light the moon suddenly bestowed on us. I don't remember if it was a full or half moon that shone, but the visibility it brought seemed unnatural. The entire landscape opened before us, as if God Himself parted the clouds and shone a lantern above our heads. Genu didn't think of the light so favorably.

"I'm sure we're not the only ones who can see better now," he said.

I wondered out loud if we were on the other side. Romania? Yugoslavia? How do you tell? There was no greeting sign welcoming us into a new country, complete with a list of hotels and restaurants. We looked around for clues. Johnny noticed tractor tracks. I analyzed the tracks and concluded the pattern to be *Românesc*. Looking back, what made me think they looked Romanian is beyond me. Maybe, like the soldier that had disappeared, my mind was betraying me.

We needed something that was undoubtedly un-Romanian. That something was only a few feet away. Lucian, perhaps attempting to make up for his mission-endangering coughing episode, trapped a strip of newspaper being carried by the wind. We excitedly gathered around it as if we were archeologists teetering on the cusp of a new discovery.

"Mark, quick! Where's your lighter?" Nick asked.

I rummaged through the pockets of my green parka and victoriously pulled out a red lighter. I cupped my hand around the flame and neared the strip of paper. I did not understand a single word. I was never more thankful for my ignorance. The only thing I knew was that beautiful strip of crusty, mud-splattered newspaper was written in the Cyrillic alphabet, the same one used by Yugoslavians.

Genu warned against false hope. "Don't get too happy just yet," he said. "It may have been blown here by the wind."

"No matter!" I snapped. "Let's move. Sitting here does us no good."

Move is what we did, until we finally arrived on the edge of the conglomeration of lights we'd been following. We stood next to each other and looked ahead.

"Now what?" someone asked.

Our aimed destination had the characteristics of a village: a narrow, semi-cobbled street between rows of quiet, flat-fronted, archaic houses.

The first house had a tall lamp post a few feet in front of it. Parked under the lamp post was a white compact sedan with a Yugoslav tag.

The village looked slightly different from the villages I was used to. For starters, the houses were further apart. In Romania, a lot of village homes shared walls. Instead of large metal gates being the only point of entry, the homes in this village had single entrance doors with steps in front. The windows were metal-framed instead of wood-framed, and larger.

"Guys, if I don't get some water, I'm going to die," Johnny said. We'd been standing around for a good minute.

We walked to the window of the closest house. I reached up and knocked on it. It didn't take long before a clean shaven, gray-haired man appeared. He swung open one of the windows and stuck his head out.

"*Voda…voda?*" I said, tipping over the imaginary glass in my hand. *Voda* was the extent of my Serbian.

"*Romunksi?*" the old man asked.

"*Da, da!*" we nodded in unison. "We are Romanians!"

He motioned for us to come around. He swung the creaking metal gates open and escorted us past the courtyard and into his home. His wife watched us as we transferred mud, both conventional and white, onto their plank floor. Like her husband, she was wearing a buttoned-up wool sweater and, typical of Eastern European villagers, her head was covered with a thick, brown scarf.

The man said something to his wife, after which she filed out through the curtained doorway. A heat reminiscent of a long lost love emanated from the wood-burning stove, which was on the other side of the room. A long and worn leather couch rested against the wall. A couple of wooden chairs stood adjacent to it and a scarred oak coffee table filled out the center.

We watched as the man poured water out of a clay jug into five bulky, plastic cups. We drank our portions as fast as we could without choking. The man smiled. Then he asked something and nodded his head, which I interpreted as *more?* We nodded. *More please.*

The man made wiping motions on his pants, then pointed toward ours. Yes, we were caked in mud, we acknowledged. He motioned for us to follow him as we were led behind the house. Outside, he turned on the water hose and handed it to me. The water was very cold.

Once we finished hosing the mud off each other, he gave us towels to dry off as best as we could. Then we were invited back inside. The woman had made a pot of hot coffee and signaled to us with an open palm to sit at the kitchen table. She poured the hot coffee into five small porcelain cups. To this day, I can taste that cup of coffee. Not only was it the perfect temperature – hot – but it was a perfect blend of coffee boldness and smoothness. I haven't had a cup of coffee as good since.

While we were basking in coffee and warmth, the old man walked off to another part of the house. Meanwhile, his wife spoke to us, and we occasionally nodded and smiled in between shivers. She seemed relaxed, undisturbed really. It was apparent we weren't the first batch of Romanians to track mud onto her floor.

Several minutes later, as we were finishing our coffee, I heard the creaking of the entrance gates. We rushed to the kitchen window. We saw the headlamps of a white sedan with blue streaks. On the side of the vehicle, I was able to make out the first three letters: M-I-L. A man in military apparel stepped out of the car, while one in civilian clothes joined him. The old man walked past us, through the kitchen door, and shook the hands of the two men.

"That lousy old man called the police on us!" Genu exclaimed. "Can you believe that? And after all that smiling."

"What do we do?" Lucian asked.

"Hold on guys," I said, not turning my attention away from the three men. "This doesn't seem like your typical police. Why would they send only one uniformed officer for five of us?"

"Maybe that's all we can see," Johnny said.

With the door open a bit, I tried to listen to the men talk. The only word I could make out was *cancelaria*, which caused me to think that the plainclothes man may have been some sort of government official. Then the military guy stepped in. As soon as he said something, the old man turned around and gestured to us to come forward.

"Should we go?" Lucian asked.

I was tired. I didn't want to run or hide anymore. We had little choice but to join the meeting, I told the guys. We were in a strange land without any money, or a single friend to run to.

We reluctantly made our way to meet the men.

"*Govorite li srpski?*" the man in the plain clothes asked.

We shook our heads. No one spoke Serbian.

Then the man in the dark gray military apparel broke in. "*Dar Românește? Vorbiți Românește*"

I wasn't sure if hearing my native tongue was a good or bad thing, especially from someone wearing a uniform. I replied that we did speak Romanian. He asked where we were from and what we were doing in this village. We confessed we were Romanians who just escaped Romania, and were looking to go to the West. He wanted to know if we had any guns or knives, any weapons of any sort. "No," we told him.

The uniformed man's name was Iosef. He lived in Yugoslavia but was ethnically Romanian. His colleague's name was Filip.

Iosef told us that we needed to go with him.

"Where are we going?" I asked.

"We need to get some paperwork filled out," he answered, "so we can get you where you want to go."

- - -

In Romania, many people have gone into official buildings to "fill out documents," only to never be heard from again.

-2-
BOZOVICI

Whenever I tell someone that I am from a village in the western Romanian county of Caraş-Severin called Bozovici, he usually assumes a small, insignificant town traveled exclusively by gravel and mud roads; a town comprised of dilapidated houses with straw roofs and a sparse citizenry who, for whatever reason, always have ashes on their faces, possess no literary skills, and get along with animals better than humans. It must be the name. It starts with *Bozo*.

For an Eastern Bloc village, the population of Bozovici wasn't so sparse. The population today, approximately 3,500, is nearly the same as it was during my childhood days of the 60's and early 70's. And as far as paved roads go, yes *and* no. The main artery road, which stretches for a couple of miles or so, was stone-paved. The few side streets, including the one we lived off of, were not. They were the type you dreaded after rain or heavy snow.

When it came to electricity, Bozovici was more sophisticated than many of the surrounding villages. Everyone had it. But aside from lamps, clocks, and radios, there wasn't much else utilizing one of the world's greatest discoveries. We didn't have televisions, microwaves, and certainly no toasters or mixers.

One may assume a village with electricity would have running water. Not Bozovici. The outhouse was the bathroom and wells dispersed throughout the village were our water source. However, Dad, whom I called Tăticu (which means "dad") was ever the innovator. He decided one late weekday afternoon to make the Hobafcovich home an exception.

"Mark," he roared across the courtyard. "Come help me with something!"

I hurried across the courtyard. Dad asked me to stretch out my arms. He loaded them with pieces of thick, plastic tubes. He then grabbed a shovel, a pickaxe, a hammer and large channel-lock pliers. We made our way out through the heavy double gates of the courtyard.

"Tăticu, what are we doing?" I asked.

I was nine. Maybe 10. Although rather tall, around six feet, my *tăticu* was not the most intimidating man. He had a very average build, and his soft, blue eyes projected anything but force. But as far as I was concerned, my dad was a work of wonder. When he spoke, everyone listened. When he listened, everyone waited for him to speak. He could do anything and knew everything. During the week he was the supervisor of the dynamite depository at the edge of the village. The Romanian government was building roads through the mountains. Instead of going around or over, someone figured it was more expedient to go *through* the mountain. And so, despite not being a member of the Communist party, Dad had the prestigious position of keeping inventory of the supplies used to blast large holes through the mountains. His other duty was to keep tabs on who was bringing and who was taking dynamite out of the depository. The position needed to be handled by a man of integrity, someone who wasn't prone to bribery and various forms of shenanigans. Dad was that man. The Communists overlooked my dad's "religious faults" and his absence of party affiliation. He was their dynamite man.

Dad tried to make life as pleasant for us as possible. We never went without anything essential. We didn't go to bed hungry or thirsty, our winter clothes were usually kept up, and nothing in the house stayed broken too long. Not that we had much that could break. And he was always looking for a way to lighten the burden of second-world living. Whatever he was working on now, I couldn't wait to see.

We walked to the top of the hill, where the well stood. I dumped the plastic pipes on the ground. Dad had already dug a little trench which stretched from the house to the well. Now he started picking at the foundation of the well until water began gushing out. One of the neighbors was passing by and noticed the gushing. "Vichente, what are you doing there?" he hollered.

"You'll see!" Dad yelled.

"You have water going everywhere. You want to get in trouble?"

"Mark, hand me that hammer," he said, no longer paying attention to the neighbor.

Our family is the only one to bear the Hobafcovich name – in the world. My shoddy investigative attempts into the origin of the family name have turned up two possibilities. The first explanation I ever heard was that some time ago my ancestors were Jews. And for reasons that most likely included avoiding some form of persecution, the family name was changed to a non-Jewish one. The other theory was proposed to my father by the village's Orthodox priest. In order to be a priest in that part of the world many generations ago, you needed to have a Slavic name. His guess was that our family had a priestly heritage. Sometime in the past, the name was concocted and applied to a future Hobafcovich so he could serve as a priest.

Whatever the source of the Hobafcovich name, Vichente Hobafcovich, father of three girls and one boy, husband of one, keeper of dynamite, informed his family that the Hobafcovichs were going to have running water.

"Running water? In the house?" My oldest sister Petra couldn't have been more excited. She carried more water than anyone.

"Not just in the house. In the barn and backyard too." Dad tried to scale back his grin by taking in a spoonful of mashed potatoes.

"Tăticu, does that mean we won't have to carry water anymore?" Mary asked. Being the second oldest, she helped Petra with the water chore.

"That's exactly what that means!" Dad answered.

"That's great! Just in time!" Chivuţa was the youngest of my sisters. Although she was three years older than me, Dad didn't want her carrying water. She was too young and frail. I had no such excuses. I was a boy in training to be a man. Carrying water was just the beginning.

We officially had the town's very first gravity-fed water system. We didn't need sophisticated pressure valves. We had topography on our side. The only valves Dad needed were shut-off valves. And the best part about it? There was no water bill. It never even occurred to Dad that we should have to pay for water. The cows, geese, ducks, lambs and chickens drank fresh water, Mom figured out other ways to utilize my sisters' assistance, and I bragged to my friends about our fancy new water system.

There weren't many ways to set families apart in Bozovici. All the houses were made of plain-colored cement and stone, and covered with roofs *not* made of straw. They were connected, as the flat front ran the length of the street, much like a townhome. The only way to tell where a new house began was by the large metal gates. They were the only option for entering and leaving a residence. Most of the houses had one lone window, some two, facing the street. Rooms on the front were not ideal if you wanted to sleep in on market day. Once a week, farmers from the surrounding villages convened in Bozovici to trade and sell goods. The roaring laughter and plodding horses were enough to wake even the soundest sleeper.

And no, the citizens of Bozovici did not walk around with dirty, ash-smudged faces. Nor were they illiterate. There were a few old timers who never learned to read, but most everyone from my parent's generation and younger knew how to read. The town had a courthouse, a few administrative firms, a police station, and even a two-story hospital.

The police station was not exactly what you might envision when you think of a police station. It was one guy; one police officer in a small building attached to the City Hall. No one knew much about him. And not many wanted to. He was a police officer. There was no visible benefit to being friends or talking to a police officer. We, especially, had reason to avoid the authorities.

- - -

My great-grandfather, Radu, fought in World War I. At one point, he spent a week in a trench next to fellow Romanians and Frenchmen. The Germans and Turks were on their last legs and so they were bombarding the enemy lines with a zealous desperation that struck fear into the hearts of those on the receiving end. Radu noticed one of the men next to him, Stefan, was oddly calm. He smiled here and there, even joked once. He asked the oddball why he wasn't afraid. Did he not have any family waiting on him back home? Did he not have a home and a profession? Or was he one of those maniacs who liked the blood and agony, who reveled amidst chaos? Stefan explained it wasn't lack of fear keeping him calm. You would have to be insane not to be afraid. And he wasn't insane, he assured Radu. It's just that he knew where he was going, should he die. Yes, he would miss his family, but he would see them again. "And besides," he added, "God is in control. I'll only die if He allows it."

Radu was intrigued. He'd never heard anyone talk like that. For the next few days in the trenches, Stefan answered question after question Great-grandfather Radu had about God, Jesus and His followers. At one point he asked Stefan how is it he knew so much about "these things" since he wasn't a priest.

"You don't need to be a priest to read the Bible," Stefan answered him.

This was news to Radu.

Sometime between firing his rifle and taking cover, Stefan managed to rummage through his sack and pull out a small black book with the words *NOUL TESTAMENT* engraved in small, gold letters on its black, worn leather. "Radu, this is a New Testament. It covers everything we talked about...*and* much more. You can read it for yourself. You can have it. Take it."

Sometime during the next week, Radu prayed with Stefan and gave his life to Jesus. Repenting of his past, he became a believer in Jesus.

Upon his return home, Radu's wife didn't know what to make of her new husband. Initially, she was afraid he would come back scarred and meaner than ever before. Instead, what she got back was a respectful, kind man. His reasoning for his new behavior was simple: he was being obedient to the instructions in the little black book with the gold letters.

Out of frustration at the absence of other believers in his village and a heartfelt desire to tell everyone about his discovery, Great-grandfather Radu went on a proselytizing mission. He told everyone he ran into about his new faith. He told them they didn't need a priest. He told them they could read about God for themselves. They could pray to Him by themselves. He told them about God's love, grace and the eternal salvation He offers. He talked about the importance of holiness and sanctification.

A lot of people dismissed him. Some people listened. Others wanted to hear more. A few wanted to get together to discuss this crazy kind of faith that can be had without a priest. Before Radu knew it, a small church had sprung up in the little village of Bania.

Great-grandfather Radu was open to having church in his home. While the adults prayed and studied the Bible, their small children played with wood blocks and dried corn cobs on the other side of the room. Those children would eventually pass the baton of this faith down to their children, one of which would be my mother.

My father, however, did not grow up in the same kind of home as my mother. His father had ties to the Orthodox church in his village. He took his membership no more seriously than most other members. It was tradition, something you did because that's what the culture and time dictated. You showed up for Easter and Christmas services, and any attendance beyond that was considered a bonus. It was ritual.

Unlike Grandfather Hobafcovich, my father could not hide under the radar of the Orthodox Church. He was discovered to have a good singing voice and asked to be an altar boy at a very young age. For years, my father sang in his local Orthodox church and was exposed to the sacred rites and liturgical practices of the Orthodox tradition.

Over time, Dad became increasingly curious regarding the religious teachings he had been hearing. He yearned for more. He wanted to know more about God, more than what the priest was offering. One day, Dad was discussing his frustration with a friend. Pouncing on the opportunity, the friend asked Dad, "Hey Vichente, have you ever read the New Testament?"

Dad, probably taken by surprise, answered, "No. No. That's only for the priest."

"No, Vichente! The New Testament should be read by people. People like you and me, not just priests."

"Are you sure?"

"Yes, I'm sure! I'll bring you one tomorrow."

Dad's friend lived up to his promise and brought him a New Testament, probably very much like the one Great-grandfather Radu received in the trenches many years ago. Shortly after reading the New Testament, Dad began bombarding his priest with questions. "What's this talk about repentance and grace? How about the part about being baptized *after* believing? And why can't we read the New Testament by ourselves?"

The priest, taken aback, asked Dad, "You wouldn't happen to be reading the New Testament, are you?"

"Yeah, actually I am," Dad answered.

"Vichente, stop reading the New Testament."

The relationship between Dad and the Orthodox Church was severed shortly afterwards. With the help of his friend, Dad was introduced to other Jesus believers in the village and surrounding towns. The group of believers was referred to as *Pocăiți*, a term that translates to Repenters. There were barely twenty of them. They gathered in homes, much like the group in Bania did a generation ago. Dad liked the informal atmosphere, by Orthodox standards, of the Repenters. He especially felt welcomed when he sensed his questions were perceived as indicators of spiritual progress instead of heretical musings.

After attending a few more meetings, Dad surrendered his life to Jesus. He was now a full-fledged, certifiable Repenter. But he wouldn't blossom spiritually until after he was drafted into the army and spent two and a half years in Cluj, a city in the heart of Transylvania. Cluj had a large, vibrant Repenter presence. He met many men and women who were further along in their spiritual journey and Biblical grounding. From them he absorbed everything he could.

By the time Dad's stint in the army was over, Vichente Hobafcovich had developed into a leader. When he returned home, he organized gatherings in the surrounding villages and taught and collaborated with other leaders in the area. It was at one of those gatherings where he met a young lady named Elena. Elena, a third generation Repenter, ultimately married Vichente and took the Hobafcovich name.

My dad, in time, became one of the lay preachers – an unpaid preacher – of the local church. Most Repenter churches throughout the country had lay preachers. The reason was because Romania's Communist government allowed only three or four men a year, in the entire country (!), to attend the one available seminary and, therefore, become ordained (certified). It was part of a larger strategy to prevent the growth of Repenters. The official State-sponsored Church was the Romanian Orthodox Church. As a result, it was lay preachers who were essentially the leaders and pastors of the churches. Since they weren't ordained in the State Church, they were not allowed by law to perform baptisms or administer the Lord's Supper. For those sacraments to be performed, Repenter churches had to summon the one ordained pastor who traveled to the surrounding regional churches for that very purpose.

- - -

Although Repenters were prohibited by authorities from gathering during the week for fear the little church would expand, my life revolved around church, and consequently, my thoughts were influenced by Biblical teaching.

Our well-kept little church sat between a shallow, rushing river and a sign that indicated its purpose, *Casa de Rugaciune* (House of Prayer). An Orthodox church, on the other side of town, claimed the rest of the town as its members. It was well known that if a Repenter church did not want to be harassed by the State, it helped to have a small congregation.

Saturdays and some Sunday afternoons were for choir and orchestra rehearsals. As soon as I could form a coherent sentence I was inducted into the children's choir. I remember singing, while my legs, still too short to rest on the worn, wood-paneled floor, dangled back and forth through the air from a hard wooden chair.

Sunday services started at nine o'clock and ended sometime after noon. The songs we sang were poorly put together and the sermons long, but that's the way it was, and many wouldn't have had it any other way, even if they knew they could.

Our humble Repenter community was tightly knit. We were pushed together by a world that did not perceive our beliefs and way of life as legitimate. The school authorities organized soccer games purposely on Sunday mornings so they could persuade us to stop attending church. Such scheduling did not affect most of the Orthodox crowd, considering they rarely attended the services anyway. Since we did not attend the soccer games, we incurred the consequences. Every Monday at school the children of *Pocăiți* received a hand-lashing from a long, fat ruler our teachers always seemed to have at their sides. Other times the lashings were just the appetizer. One day I was dragged to the front by my ear, where the teacher slammed my head against the chalkboard for not "coming to support" the Bozovici soccer team. Moreover, there was the constant dose of verbal abuse bestowed upon us by most teachers, and the inevitable following of example by other students. Many times I came home upset and confused.

We Repenters clung to each other wherever there was more than one of us, almost by default. Even if we didn't like each other on Sundays, in class we were best friends.

- - -

Contrasting ideologies were brewing. At school I was being indoctrinated with atheist ideals completely opposite of what I'd grown up hearing at home. I was basically told everything I believed about life was wrong. God was not real, I was assured. He was imaginative, a fairy tale indicative of ignorant and unsophisticated epochs. Wishful thinking, really. Humanism had arrived. It was time to do away with the superstitions and get on board with progress.

Some of the things the teachers said made sense to me. Not only had I never seen God, but neither had anyone I knew, including people who assured me He existed. However, despite the confusion, there was one thing I was convinced of, the only thing I could count on: *Mom and Dad would never lie to me*.

Needless to say, a stew of mistrust and confusion bubbled up into my curious and fragile mind. Who was right? Who was wrong? What was really going on? My seesaw of mistrust was leaning against my teachers and the other cruel people who made life harder on me.

I remember eating lunch one Sunday afternoon and asking Mom why Dad wasn't around. "He's at church," I was told.

"But we just came from church."

I already knew what he was doing. We may have been young, but my friends and I were already passing around secret information. Although we just had a baptism service in the morning, there was another one after everyone left. It was a *secret* baptism. It was for people who wanted to get baptized but weren't allowed.

Anytime a baptism service was planned, the church leaders were obligated to give the list of those who wanted to get baptized to the local authorities. In turn, the authorities made sure everyone who wanted to get baptized was already part of a Repenter family. If they weren't, the traveling preacher was forbidden from baptizing them.

The fear of authorities was not enough to prevent anyone determined enough from being baptized. And it certainly didn't hold Dad back from being an accomplice to the baptizing of prohibited citizens. Someone figured the best way to reconcile the realities was by baptizing the forbidden persons when no one was looking; after everyone went home and the building was locked. That's when the new believers unrelated to Repenters came out of the shadows to be baptized.

I didn't like that my dad had to sneak around to help baptize people. It didn't seem right. I didn't like being ridiculed by my teachers for something my parents believed in and forced me to take part in. I didn't think life should be that way.

Something was wrong. There had to be a better way. That much I knew.

- - -

I remember having a friend who liked drawing the Chevrolet car's "bow tie." He liked cars. He hadn't seen many. But somewhere, he once saw a picture of a cherry red, late 1960's convertible Camaro. He talked about it as if he'd seen a spaceship. Since he wasn't good enough to draw the spaceship from memory, he drew the iconic bow tie on the grill instead.

Dad usually subscribed to one or two magazines at the beginning of each year. He'd fill out a little card with the joy of a child who was ordering toys. One year in particular, maybe 1972, I remember coming home to find a copy of one of those magazines on the table. Before I glanced at it, I already decided I was going to dismiss it as just another mundane magazine that featured things I could care less about. That was usually the case. But the cover caused me to do a double take. It was a picture of the 1956 Summer Olympics in Melbourne, Australia. The image was an aerial view of a crammed and grandiose stadium. It wasn't just spectators that filled the stadium, but athletes from every country in the world. They were dressed nice and looked so happy…and free. I'm not sure what caused me to think they looked free. Maybe it was their smiles. Maybe it was the bright countenance of the picture; the sun shone brighter in Australia. Maybe I imagined everyone in that city had running water and Camaros. Kids there drew the entire car, not just the bow tie. They probably weren't harassed in school for not going to a soccer game. People who looked so happy probably never had to perform secret baptisms.

There, indeed, existed a different world. I was sure of it now. And it wasn't a worse world, as I'd been told. The image in that magazine reinforced what I wanted to believe all along. At school they told us the West, especially America, was poor and fraught with violence; unemployment was staggeringly high, people waited in line for food, and riots were an everyday occurrence. We should thank our lucky stars we were living in the Promised Land. But as I stared at the picture of the packed stadium in a free country, I became convinced life was better off on the other side of the fence.

I made up my mind that one day I would leave Romania. I told Dad later that week. "Tăticu, one of these days, when I grow up, I'm going to send you a postcard from the other side of the fence!"

Everyone knew there was a fence keeping Romanians in. You couldn't just leave because it was something that you wanted. You had to jump through umpteen hoops and walk 10 miles on a wire just to be considered to be allowed out. Although I didn't know why, I knew something about the fence wasn't right. One day I asked one of my teachers, "If Romania is so good, why is there a fence keeping us in?"

"The fence is not to keep you in. It is to keep others out," the teacher said proudly and grinned.

I didn't dare say anything else. I was too scared to voice my true thoughts. One day, I'm going to leave this place.

Perhaps I expected Dad to be proud of my traveling aspirations. I imagined he'd put the exotic postcard I would send him on his wall, and when people came over, he'd point to it and grin, telling them his son lives Not In Romania.

But Dad thought my dream was nothing more than the empty ramblings of an undeveloped mind. "Don't speak of childish things," he said sharply. "You don't know what you're talking about."

Although Dad had come a long way from his impoverished upbringing, and was in many ways a pioneer, getting out of Romania was not something he considered feasible. I might as well have told him I was going to ride a unicorn out of Romania. He had only heard stories of brutal capture, harsh prison sentences and inhumane labor camp conditions as the fate of those who tried to leave the motherland. He knew of no one who made it to the other side. To risk your livelihood for something so impossible made little sense to him. And besides, Dad had already moved up the socioeconomic ladder. Growing up, his family was poor as a church mouse. It wasn't uncommon for his family to go days eating nothing but cabbage soup and porridge. But thanks to his uncle marrying well, combined with a list of tragedies, Dad acquired quite a bit of land. Later on, the Communists took Dad's land to the collectivization, but were generous enough to allow his family to work it and keep a hefty 30 percent of the fruit of their labor. I suppose being allowed to keep 30 percent of something made sense if you grew up having 100 percent of nothing.

Dad didn't see it. He had reached the pinnacle of his dreaming. A world beyond the only one he knew of was out of his range of vision.

Ironically, such an outlook wasn't always the case with Dad's uncle, the one who'd married well. Knowing my aspirations, he told me how he once had a dream of going to a better land. He wearily looked at me through his dim eyes and said, "Back in those days, all you had to do was take a train to France, which wasn't prohibited, where American ships were waiting to take immigrants to America. They couldn't get enough immigrants for all the work there was to be done."

"You mean you could just show up?"

He sighed. "It was that easy, Mark. It's hard to believe now. They had free immigration back then. And no one here forced you to stay in the country either. Just show up on American shores, and in no time you would be working…and keeping the labor of your hands."

"Why didn't you go?" I asked.

"I wanted to, but I was the oldest. I had to take care of my siblings. I fought the idea long and hard, too long. Before I knew it, it was too late."

Dad's uncle, the one I'd been named after, was the only person I knew who shared my vision for a better life.

- - -

Even though Dad cared very little for my exodus ambitions, he inadvertently contributed fuel to the fire.

He had a short-wave radio on which he listened to a Romanian preacher from America. One day, when no one was around, I started messing around with it. I was looking for something. I wasn't sure what it was. While going back and forth between static and hints of clear narration, I came across a sound I'd never heard before. I gently played with the knob until I got the signal as clear as possible.

The station was dubbed Radio Free Europe. Out of the little crackling speaker blared a raspy singing voice that tended to burst into wild screaming without warning. It was the strangest thing. I'd never heard anything like it. The band that accompanied this coarse-sounding, crazy woman was able to produce a sound like that of a melodic machine gun. I later learned such a sound was produced by guitars plugged into amplifiers turned really loud. I had heard of electric guitars. Now I was assured they existed, and musical machine guns were what they sounded like. The thump of the percussion section reminded me of a rumbling train.

The screaming singer's name, Cornell Chiriac, the disc jockey, informed me, was Janis Joplin. Her band was called Big Brother. The song was "Piece of my Heart." He informed his Romanian listeners all the way from Munich that Janis was born in a place she knew was not for her. She didn't fit in. She didn't like it there. She had dreams of singing blues music. So she got up and moved to San Francisco where people who understood her dreams lived, where she might have the opportunity to fulfill those dreams.

DJ Chiriac was a Romanian who fled years ago and now lived in free West Germany. He ultimately introduced my friends and me to other influential American rock stars, guys like Bob Dylan and Jimi Hendrix. They pursued their dreams and left for places they believed would nourish their ambitions. That was his thing. Chiriac not only told us about the musicians, he talked about the songs. He translated certain lines. He gave us the meaning of a song…if there was one. He especially informed listeners of the meanings of songs which had to do with freedom. Chiriac loved jazz music. He reminded his audience that jazz was music birthed out of freedom, the first music to come from blacks in the United States after their emancipation. Freedom talk infused all of his *Metronome* shows; freedom of choice, freedom of ideas and freedom to do what you want.

I found what I was looking for when I started aimlessly turning that little knob. Radio Free Europe did to me exactly what it was created to do: plant the seed of doubt against all things Communist in the minds and hearts of those of us living behind the red Iron Curtain. Funded by the CIA at the time, Radio Free Europe had a huge budget, and they flaunted their high-quality shows and DJs at every opportunity. The Americans, like the Russians, thought the Cold War would be won with the weapons of ideas.

I'd been shot by Radio Free Europe.

- - -

The possible priestly heritage in my family tree and the Repenter pioneers on both sides, along with the endless hours spent at choir rehearsals and taking in Biblical discourse didn't do it. And even my dad being one of the preachers of the church in Bozovici didn't inspire me to stick to the pattern.

In reality, I wasn't a Repenter. I wasn't Orthodox. The ridicule I received at school was unwarranted. I was guilty only by association. I wasn't an atheist either. I just wanted to be free. I wanted to have fun, to do whatever I thought I should be allowed to do and not be punished for it. I was sick of restraints. My church told me what not to do, my government told me what I couldn't do, my teachers told me what I did was all wrong. Wherever I turned I heard *no*.

NO!

I was sick of it. I would have to leave for a place far, far away. A Yes place.

Although I wasn't sure exactly how I would ever leave Romania, I would start by leaving Bozovici.

-3-

PUTTING THE BAND TOGETHER

Eight of us shared the dormitory of the technical school in Reşiţa. We each slept in a single, uniform bed, and we all shared the same military-style bathroom. A long coat rack hung on the wall by the main entrance. Shoes and books were kept neatly beside every bed.

Half the kids in the room were like me, naive and wide-eyed boys looking for something new and exciting, thankful to have escaped the constraints of the village.

I did not consider the school in Bozovici an option. Aside from wanting to leave Bozovici, I wanted to learn something more on the technical side, like electricity. When I discovered Dad's radio long ago I developed a tendency to hoard any electrical components that I found. Sometimes I built other contraptions with them, many of which did not work. Most of the classes I needed in order to have a career in electricity were taught only in the city. And since the dorms were subsidized by the State, there was little stopping me.

At first, my parents suggested I stay home a few more years. Their reservations were probably based on how they thought I might deal with the temptations of "the world." They must've reasoned a boy looking for adventure as bad as I had been was likely to cliff-dive the first chance that he got. Only God knew in what shallow waters I would land.

Sensing my determination, my parents conceded and let me leave Bozovici. On the day of departure, they gave me a final spiel about the tools of the devil. Then they hugged me and waved until the bus had driven out of sight.

I was 14 and on my own – just a skinny country kid on his way to the big city.

- - -

I was just Mark. Not Mark the Repenter freak anymore.

Few things are sweeter to a teenager than fitting in. And as it turned out, I was good at it. I made friends quickly and wasted little time venturing out into the world.

"Hey Mark, we're going to *Casa de Cultura*. You want to come?" one of my roommates asked.

"What's that?"

"A discotheque!" he answered.

"I've never been before," I told him.

"That's exactly why you need to come. Let's go! I'll introduce you to some girls."

"Alright. You've convinced me."

The bass got louder with every step that brought me closer to the culture-harboring house. Kids my age were filing into a plain, rectangular building from all sides. I showed my student identification card to one of the officers at the entrance, paid my three *lei*, and joined them.

A group of boys were congregating around the lone Pac Man video game machine in the far right corner. Some people were dancing, and others were lined against the wall, smoking and talking. There was a bar but no alcohol. Unlike the discotheques in the West, ours were sponsored by the State as a means to keep us out of trouble. The music struggling out of the few speakers was foreign to me. It was certainly not rock 'n roll, or anything I'd heard on Radio Free Europe.

My friend motioned for me to follow him to the bar, from where he'd been waved over by a couple of girls.

"Mark, this is Cornelia." He made no mention of her friend, the girl he had already wrapped his arm around.

"Hi Mark." The glare from the lights spotlighted the unnatural redness of her lips.

"Mark's from Bozovici," my friend blabbed.

"Never heard of it."

Cornelia would be the first in a modest line of similar girls I would meet in the coming years. Her blue polyester pants clung to her for dear life. Her blouse seemed to have been bought before it was finished and her lengthy dark hair shone as if it were wet.

She lit a cigarette. "Would you like one?" She stretched out an open pack in my direction.

I probably looked like a child who'd just been asked to pet a strange dog, staring at the outstretched arm while the voices in my head were battling it out. *Take the cigarette! Don't do it Mark.*

At first, I didn't like cigarettes. They made me nauseous. But I learned to like smoking. At first, I was a little uneasy about the clubs and the made-up girls. They made me nervous. But I learned to like them. And they liked me too. On top of dressing different, they talked and thought different. They knew of Bob Dylan. They danced. They didn't always wait for you to make the first move. They were at ease. These were no Bozovici girls. These were the cliffs my parents were afraid I'd jump off.

- - -

Reșița had one Repenter church, a Baptist one. I had no interest in visiting. Sundays, along with Thursdays, were discotheque days. We had classes six days a week. I wasn't going to spend my one day off going to church. However, there was a certain man who did attend that church.

"Mark, there's someone outside the gate asking for you," I was told.

"Who is it?"

"I didn't ask. But he asked for you by name. You're the only Hobafcovich I know," the boy said.

I put my book down, slipped on a jacket and shoes, and started outside.

On the other side of the gate there stood a dark-haired man, possibly in his late twenties. He looked familiar.

"Mark? Mark Hobafcovich?" he asked.

"Yes, that's me." I put my hand out. "You look familiar. How do I know you?"

"I'm Isaiah." He shook my hand. "I believe we met at your sister's wedding. I'm a friend of her husband's."

"Oh! Now I remember. What do you—?"

"Mark, how long are you going to stray?"

"Excuse me—"

"How long are you going to keep drifting away, Mark?"

"Isaiah, can you tell me what you've heard?"

"I've heard enough. You know better. Stop now and turn to God."

The guy was stern, and somewhat inept at the art of communication. He was convinced of my iniquitous activities and seemed displeased with them.

He tried to talk to me and elaborate on what he knew of my wicked ways, but I wasn't particularly interested in hearing it. Why did I need him to inform me of my activities? Who knew better than I what I'd been up to?

Although Isaiah's tongue-lashing would not convince me of anything at the time, his words would haunt me for years to come. They especially rung loud and clear a year and a half later when disaster would strike the country.

At first I thought someone was clowning around and shaking the bed rail at my feet. But there was no one there. Yet the shaking persisted. I turned around and noticed the boy to my right was looking around stupidly just like me, except he looked more scared than confused. I solved the mystery and was about to exclaim to everyone what was happening when I heard the boys in the bathroom shouting," Earthquake! Earthquake!"

One of them came running out with only a towel around his waist, laughing hysterically. "Everyone under your bed! It's going to get you! We're all going to die!" he hollered, following it with maniacal laughter as he jumped up and down on the bed. That boy was always a little strange.

Although the only damage the 1977 Vrancea earthquake did in Reșița was shatter a few plates and baffle a roomful of teenage boys, it did bring the eastern part of the country to its knees. Approximately 1,600 people died and over 10,000 were seriously hurt. We were glued to the lone television as we watched footage of the rubble in the capital, Bucharest. Buildings were flattened like stacks of dirty, broken dishes. Corpses, and parts of corpses, were found continuously for days. People covered in ashes, dust and blood walked about confused and terror-stricken. On-site workers, medics and crane operators were scarce in comparison to the need. Among the dead were national actors. The president canceled his out-of-country trip in order to visit the damaged sites.

Isaiah's words, "Mark, how long?" echoed in my head as I realized how fragile life was. One moment you could be a rich somebody sleeping in a fancy apartment in the capital and another moment your life could be crushed. And then what?

What happens after that?

I knew what happened afterwards. That's why I wanted Isaiah out of my head. I didn't like what he was making me think about. His words frequently reverberated as I struggled with my identity in the years to come. The idea of turning to God, a concept I didn't even fully understand, loomed in the background of every existential conversation I would have over the years.

How long? Until when, Mark?

It would be some time before those questions were answered.

- - -

For a minute, I was distracted. The partying and the female attention, in combination with a career, had almost put to rest my dream of leaving the country. Almost.

The partying eventually lost its thrill; it no longer provided the escapist effect it once had. Now I felt trapped all the time. No matter how hard I worked, no matter what degree I attained and how good a high-power electrician I would ever become, I could never reach my full potential. My full potential was completely dependent on living in a free society. I was not even close.

Even if I could somehow learn to be content working and living in Romania, as so many had, the fact that I could lose it all in a bureaucratic instant, as my dad or his uncle did, was something I could not get over. Furthermore, almost everyone I knew had somebody – a friend, uncle, father, or brother – who had "disappeared." And very few were guilty of conventional crimes. It wasn't uncommon for people to be taken to jail or the labor camps purely based on the word of an informer, or the suggestion of someone in the Communist party. Fair trials, in Romania, were as common as the unicorn Dad believed I would have to saddle if I was ever to get out.

The reality of the labor camps on the Danube Canal especially hit home when my younger cousin, Dani, returned home in a coffin. Like so many before him, Dani died working on the Canal. Although most workers on the Canal were prisoners, there were quite a few whose military orders included Canal labor. It just so happened that most enlisted army men who worked on the Canal "coincidentally" came from Repenter families.

The Danube Canal project had been shut down for almost 20 years before it was restarted in 1973, at the behest of our scepter-owning leader, Nicolae Ceaușescu. One of the problems with the project was the inferior tools the workers were forced to use. Most of the terrain was extremely hard and rocky, yet the forced laborers were given only shovels and pickaxes.

And just *who* were these prisoner laborers? Anyone the *Securitate* – the Romanian secret police, a spying and arresting entity that answered only to the president – deemed "dangerous" or "undesirable" to the State. Undesirables included farmers who attempted to resist collectivization, anti-government activists, incompliant religious leaders, Zionist Jews, common criminals and anyone caught trying to escape the country (who were usually filed under at least one of the mentioned groups). Once a prisoner was assigned a digging section, he was put in a brigade, which was usually run by a common criminal, who was encouraged to use violence to get the most out of his crew. These men were animals.

If a beating wasn't incentive enough to work hard, there was also the food factor. It wasn't unusual for prisoners to be fed only a small bowl of cabbage soup and a piece of moldy bread a day. Many prisoners resorted to eating mice and grass. And you might as well forget about hygiene and medical attention. Tuberculosis and every other form of disease spread through the filthy, crowded, frosty cells like a shadow over a dark city. Unless you had information the State deemed valuable, there was little expense allocated for your medical treatment. The State's mantra was sobering: *you are here because you are a nuisance to the State. And if the eyes of the world weren't on us, you'd easily be exterminated.* The Canal was referred to as the "graveyard of the Romanian bourgeoisie" by the authorities. They got the graveyard part right.

They told us Dani's death was an "unfortunate accident." We weren't so convinced. Even if it were close to true, we would never know.

Years after Dani's "accident" we would have to bury another family member. One of my sister's brothers-in-law, Vasile, was killed in a car accident while traveling the country, preaching. He'd been "asked" by authorities to stop his proselytizing efforts many times before. Although he'd officially been killed in a car accident, my family, upon receiving his body, noticed a bullet hole…in his head.

The mistrust started at the top and trickled down to the lowest levels of government. Most Romanians lost the split-second adoration they might have had for our head of state once they realized communism was not all it was talked up to be. We saw only two equalities: the poverty among the people, and the corruption of the people in charge.

Ceaușescu, who sometimes referred to himself as the Genius of the Carpathians, was the president and maniacal brains behind the machine that ruled the Socialist Republic of Romania. His wife, Elena, was reported to have much input regarding policies as well.

For a brief minute, Ceaușescu was viewed by the West as the Eastern Bloc darling. When the Soviet-led Warsaw Pact invaded Czechoslovakia in 1968, Ceaușescu publicly denounced the invasion and made it clear Romania would have no part of it. The West loved him for that. Although I was young at the time, I remember the awesome sight and sound of Soviet planes, on their way to Czechoslovakia, roaring high above our garden in Bozovici. Ceauşescu's public stance was probably part of a ploy to gain financial favor from the West with one hand, while with the other one behind his back he continued to perpetuate Romania's downward descent by working deals with a Who's Who list of dictators and terrorist leaders. Some contemporary sources claimed that Romania wasn't even asked to partake in the invasion. The uproar was just an act.

The most important day in Romania was January 26. Radio and television stations offered nothing but exaggerated praise for our dear *Conducător*. People turned out for the national parades in droves, as they exerted every muscle in their faces to keep their smiles as wide and prolonged as possible. They beat their palms red and exhausted their vocal chords to demonstrate their appreciation for the man they voted in year after year (never mind there was no one else ever on the ballot). Few dared not show up and appreciate. Our Dear Leader's birthday was the greatest day on earth. It would be a shame to end up picking rocks and eating moldy bread because you may have *appeared* to be indifferent to the abundance and blessings that Ceauşescu bestowed on your life.

There were three types of people in Romania. The masses (the status quo who were too paralyzed by fear and intimidation to question the system), those who used the system for their personal gain at the expense of others, and we very few, who couldn't take it anymore.

- - -

I didn't talk much about leaving for fear of informants, one of the *Securitate's* main tools of control. Informants were either bribed, threatened or they volunteered in return for favors and money. Being that I was surrounded by people I didn't know in a city of tens of thousands, I had to be careful in whom I confided. If I was ever going to take a step toward leaving the country, I had to wait until the right opportunity came along. What that would look like, I had no idea. For the time being, I would have to play the game and smile.

After going back and forth between Reșița and Timișoara for school and fun, I eventually graduated and began working in the high-voltage electrical station in Reșița. My main job was to maintain the bulky and intimidating apparatuses responsible for powering the city. In my back pocket I always kept the words of my favorite instructor: "Guys, in this field you only get one shot." The first time he made that statement he followed it up with slides of charred corpses.

Although I thought it might be something I'd enjoy, I can't say the reality panned out. It was a boring job.

I was bored.

And then along came Genu.

One chilly November day, I was in my tiny, one-room apartment reading the newspaper and listening to the radio when my concentration was disturbed by quick, thunderous knocking.

"Mark! Mark Hobafcovich!"

It was a desperate tone. A little bit scary.

I put my left eye over the peephole. A stocky, blonde-haired fellow in a black winter coat fidgeted closely on the other side. Sweat beads were running down his forehead. This wasn't the first time I'd seen this guy.

I first met Genu when he visited his brother in our dorm a few years back. The second time was only a couple of weeks ago. He noticed and stopped me on the street. We chatted a few minutes. He asked me where I lived. Thinking nothing of it, I told him. I even pointed out the entrance to the building.

Now it seemed he wanted to come in. Am I part of a scheme of sorts? I wondered.

"Quickly! Shut the door." Genu slammed the door behind him.

"Nice to see you again, Genu. I'm doing well. Thanks for asking. And you?"

He paced on the linoleum entrance square.

"Should I be expecting anyone else?" I looked through the peep-hole.

"Shhhh! Not so loud." He placed his right ear on the door. "Do you hear anyone?"

I hesitantly rested my left ear on the door. We were facing each other. "No. Not really."

I walked over to turn the radio down.

"What's going on?" I asked.

No answer. Genu still had his ear on the door.

I asked again.

"They're after me!" he whispered back without looking at me.

"Who's after you?"

"The *Securitate!*"

I could hear plenty of footsteps going back and forth in the hall. It was Sunday. Lots of people were coming and going.

"What happened?" I pulled out a chair and offered it.

He was reluctant to step away from the door. Only after a minute did he breathe out and sit down.

"I was sleeping when someone knocked on my door. I looked to see who it was and saw two police officers. One was taller and skinnier than the other. I put on my clothes and shoes and jumped out the window—"

"You jumped out the window?"

"What? No. I climbed down the emergency stairs."

"Oh."

"Anyway. While I was running I looked back to see if anyone was chasing me. I think I saw the tall one chasing me. I guess the fat one stayed behind, probably to go through my things. But I lost the tall one too. He was too slow for me."

"Why are they after you?" I clasped my hands together.

"Can I get a glass of water? I'm really thirsty. I've been running and hiding all day." He wiped his brow.

I poured a glass of water from the faucet and handed it to him. "Are you hungry?"

"Starving."

I took the block of cheese and a loaf of bread off the shelf and set them on the table. I shuffled through a small stack of plates and knives. Genu started slicing the cheese before I sat down. Then he tore off a piece of bread.

"Genu, why are they after you?"

"Oh yeah." He motioned for me to allow him to finish swallowing.

"Me and a friend made plans to go to the other side of the fence. We had everything in place. We agreed to meet at the train station when it was time to go."

"Okay." I nodded. He was finishing off a bite.

DEFECTOR

"But instead of going to the spot we were supposed to meet, I waited on the other side of the station, where I could see the bench without being seen. After some time it looked like my friend wasn't going to show up. I was just about to leave on my own when I saw three police officers arrest a blonde-haired man who had just sat on the bench. That's when it hit me!" He pounded the table, causing the empty cups I had left gathering to wobble. "The scum ratted me out! They thought the blonde man was me!" He guzzled the last of the water.

"Hmm."

"Mark, I'm not going to prison. Do you know what they do to people like me? I've heard stories. I'll die before going to prison!"

He must've forgotten we were supposed to be quiet. He was practically yelling.

I wondered why Genu came to me. He barely knew me. For a man on the run for his life he sure was risking a lot. He didn't know that I'd thought about leaving. Did he?

"So, what was the plan?" I asked. "How were you guys going to get out?"

"The original plan was to leave by Toager. That's where I served as a border soldier when I was in the army. We were going to walk the railroad tracks to get in the border zone. Once there, we could cross into Yugoslavia and then go to a U.N. refugee camp in Austria."

"So what now?"

"My life is over here. I need to disappear. There's a cabin in the mountains. I'll probably hide out there and leave when things cool off."

In the background, coming out of two four-inch speakers, barely disturbing the near silence, the words were as clear as though the speakers were blaring and twice the size: "*Freedom's just another word for*

44

nothing left to lose..." We didn't need to know English. DJ Chiriac told us more about that song than any other. Chiriac told us more about that line than any other in the song.

Genu and I looked at each other in silence. The DJ who introduced so many of us to people like Janis Joplin and the song she'd made famous, "Me and Bobby McGee." The Romanian who riled up the youth with his anti-Communist rants and his ideas of freedom, had died years ago. Even though he was in Munich at the time, the *Securitate* still managed to assassinate him. But the thoughts he planted in the minds of his listeners were alive and well.

Janis Joplin's faint voice put things into perspective. Genu certainly had nothing left to lose. And me? What would I lose if I lost everything I had? What would I lose if my entire life, as it was, was shattered?

Nothing. I would lose nothing.

"I want to do it," I said, breaking the silence.

"Do what?"

"Leave. Escape. Flee to the other side of the fence."

"Are you serious?" he asked.

"I've been thinking about this for years. Lately, it's been all I think about."

"I knew I came to right place." He smiled.

I grabbed a map off the shelf and pushed the cheese and bread to the edge of the table. I unfolded the map.

"So, where's Toager?"

- - -

I couldn't sleep for nights to come. In my younger days, I daydreamed for hours about swimming pools, sports cars and records galore. Now here I was, a big boy with a revived childhood dream. I was getting out of Romania. I believed it. And although I had no idea of what lurked on the ambiguous other side, I wouldn't have traded that hope for a million dollars.

After two weeks, it became obvious Genu wasn't going to leave my apartment. I worked, and he lounged around the apartment, trying to stay out of trouble. When he wasn't hitting on my female neighbors, he was cooking and keeping the apartment clean; soup here and there, maybe some sort of meat and vegetable medley. He worked with whatever I could find at the sparsely-supplied market. He didn't put much love in the food, just the kind of frantic experimental touch expected from him. Some days the food was better than others. Regardless, it was nice to have hot food waiting when I got home. Besides, we had more important things to worry about.

One day after work I asked him if he knew anyone else who might want to defect with us. I figured there was safety in numbers. He was already ahead of me.

"I do. We're going to meet him in a few days," he answered.

"Who?"

"A guy named Nick."

"Do you trust him?" I asked.

"He's already tried escaping once."

We waited until the sun went down before we visited Nick. Even in the dark, Genu kept his head down and his hoodie over his eyes. I remarked that it made him look like a man with something to hide.

"I *am* a man with something to hide," he retorted.

- - -

No sooner was the entrance door shut that Genu blurted out the reason for our visit. "Hey, we're going to the other side. You want to come?" It appeared Genu wasn't keen on small talk.

The new guy didn't flinch. He didn't need time to think about it. "Yes," he answered as soon as the door behind us was shut. It's as if he knew what we were going to ask him.

"Who is *he*?" Nick asked, pointing to me.

"This is Mark. He's a good guy."

I put out my hand.

"Hey, Mark. How do you know this character?" Nick asked.

"He came to hide at my place a couple of weeks ago. I've been stuck with him ever since," I explained.

"Is the *Securitate* after you?" Nick asked.

Genu nodded. "The scum I was supposed to escape with was an informer. He sold me out."

"I can't say I'm surprised. I never would've trusted that guy in the first place," Nick said.

"Yeah, you trusted some *other* guy who turned you in," Genu said.

"Point taken. Have a seat guys."

Nick's apartment was tidy and small like mine. The walls were gray, across the floors stretched worn linoleum, and the only evidence of an inhabiting soul was a bulky reel-to-reel tape player set against the wall. I didn't see any tape reels.

We sat on a soft couch and Nick dragged a small, plastic chair from the kitchen. He sat across from us.

At nearly 30, Nick was a few years older than us. He had a son who stayed with his mother. He was slim. He occasionally adjusted his thinning dark-brown hair back in place whenever it slipped out of line. Although he spoke fast, as if fearing he might not be allowed to finish his sentence, there was a composed confidence and calmness in his manner.

Nick said if he went with us he'd have to wait two weeks.

"Why?" we asked.

"I'm on probation. If I disappear and miss my meeting, they might start looking for me and blow the whole thing open."

"Fair enough."

"I know a few other guys who want to go," Nick added.

"Who?" Genu and I asked.

"One is my nephew. We can definitely trust him. The other one is a trucker friend who has also tried escaping and done his time for it. His name is Florin. This time we're going to get it right."

Nick's determination encouraged me. I had no question he was coming with us. He already had plans to go before we even arrived. He seemed like a great addition to the crew.

Lucian was Nick's 18-year-old nephew. Stocky and average height, Lucian had matching brown hair and eyes. When Nick presented the plan, Lucian said that as long as his uncle was coming, he was on board. He spoke softly and cautiously, as though weighing every thought before releasing it to the world.

"Why do you want to go to the other side?" I asked Lucian.

"Well," Lucian's eyes rolled up, as if searching for the perfect answer and said, "the same reason you do. I want to do what I want. I don't want to work the rest of my life in that factory. I hate that place. They say it's the best place for me. I don't think so. It's not the best place. Who are they to say what's best for me?"

Then there was the barrel-chested, rough-looking Florin. Years ago he had been caught just yards before crossing the border. He was sentenced to work on the Canal and had permanent scars on his back to prove the welcoming he got when he arrived. Somewhere in his mid to late thirties, Florin would be the oldest in the crew. Florin drove an 18-wheeler truck. He knew the country well and could come in handy should the plan get messy. But getting Florin to talk was like getting a pig to stay still three days before Christmas.

"What do you think?" I asked him after Genu revealed the plan.

"It's good," he said.

"So you're in?" Nick asked.

"Yes."

The last guy we visited was more Lucian's friend than Nick's. He was a youthful, trendy fellow I dubbed Boots. Nick, Lucian and I met him in a cafe. I immediately noticed his expensive and snazzy Italian leather boots. As a consequence, I never remembered his name. I called him *Boots* instead. Soon everyone was calling him "Boots."

When we told Boots the plan and asked if he was in, he tightened his lips and rolled down his eyes. "I'll do it. I'll come," he finally said.

"Are you sure?" I asked. "You don't seem so sure?"

"No, I'm sure. I've had enough of this place. Just tell me when." He lit up a cigarette.

"As soon as I'm off probation," Nick informed him. "Are you okay with that?" He stared at him intensively.

"Yes, that's fine."

Once you reveal someone the plan to escape, you can't take it back. Genu clarified this unwritten rule one night after I relayed the meeting details to him.

"If Boots gets the idea that we're not interested in having him as part of the crew, we don't know what he's capable of doing. He might tell the authorities out of spite," he said.

- - -

The boys and I agreed we should go somewhere secluded to talk about our escape plan. The only problem was Florin had a delivery to make to Bucharest that weekend and couldn't make it. He did, however, encourage us to go. He even offered us his car...I guess.

The day of the meeting finally arrived. Being as I was the only one with a driver's license, I was in charge of the key and the car. I realized Florin never actually gave me the keys to his Dacia 1100. It bothered me that he could be so absent-minded, and it angered me that I didn't realize it until it was too late. He had already left town.

But we weren't going to be thwarted. The five of us walked to his apartment anyway, hoping he may have left the key somewhere around or in his car. We looked on top of the tires, underneath the car, in between the grill, inside the wheels. No sign of the key.

What to do now?

"He gave us permission, right?"

"Yeah...where are you going with this Nick?" I looked at him suspiciously.

"He just forgot to give us the key. But we still have permission to take the car. So, let's take it anyway," Nick said.

"Maybe he changed his mind," Lucian suggested.

"He didn't!" Nick snapped.

"Maybe he never really meant to lend it anyway," Genu cut in.

"Guys, stop the nonsense! Let's just break in, get this thing running, and drive up to *Muntele Semenic* like we planned!"

Break in? We all looked at each other. What did we know about breaking into cars?

Nick pushed open the driver vent window. He snaked his left arm through and unlocked the driver-side door. He stepped in the car and rummaged through the console until he found a flathead screwdriver. He ducked under the dashboard, removed some plastic pieces, messed around with some wires, and started the car.

"Let's go, boys!" he said, winking.

"Where did you learn how to do that?" Boots asked.

"Yeah. Where?" I was also interested.

Our troubles weren't over yet. On the way to the resort, I hit someone with the car; a person on foot. It was more like I tapped him. The man popped out of nowhere on a dark and winding road. I stopped immediately. What choice did I have? He was blocking the narrow road. We all hopped out of the car.

"I'm so sorry! Are you alright?" I ran over to the man.

He looked himself over as he struggled to his feet. "Yes. I think I'm alright. You boys aren't drunk, are you?"

"No!"

"Are you the driver?" he asked.

"Yes," I told him.

"Do you have a driver's license?"

"Yes."

"Let me see it," he demanded.

The man was clearly going to be alright.

"He doesn't have to show you his license!" Nick clamored. "You came out of nowhere!"

"It's dark and I just rounded the corner," I said.

"Maybe you're the one who's drunk!" Nick continued. "Walking in the middle of the street like that."

"I work for the military base down the street," he pointed. He pulled his I.D. out of his coat pocket. I moved in to inspect it. It was dark and hard to see.

"Look, sir, we didn't mean anything…it's just that…well, you know. You never know who's trying to hustle you." I was going to have to smooth this over.

"I understand. Now license please?"

I pulled out my license papers. He took out a small flashlight, examined the paper, and then me.

"Sir, if we could just put this whole thing behind us, we'd much appreciate it. We're on our way to visit a sick comrade and we don't want to get there too late."

As Nick was speaking, Genu suggested we should give the man some money, hoping he'd shut up and go away. We came together and quickly put together 1,000 *lei*. "Here, take this. Please accept our apologies."

The middle-aged man flipped through the notes and looked up as he stuffed them in his coat pocket. "Comrades, be careful and go visit your friend."

- - -

We could've done without the trip to the *Muntele Semenic* resort. We only discussed the plan once, and it wasn't anything so complex as to require an entire weekend.

"The basic plan, boys, is to leave by the western border and aim for the U.N. refugee camp in Austria," Genu reiterated. "We want to cross the border as close to Christmas as possible. The guards will most likely be distracted, and if we're lucky, drunk and passed out. Any questions?"

There were no objections and only a few questions. Overall, everyone thought the plan sounded fine. It's not as if anyone had another one in mind. The rest of the time we used to piddle around the lobby and chase girls. I had to keep an eye on the guys, lest they were stupid enough to reveal our defecting intentions as part of an attempt to impress the ladies.

When we got back to Florin's apartment, we found out he had called the police.

"You did what? Florin, have you lost your mind? Don't you remember saying, 'Hey guys, you can borrow my car?' Because we do!" Nick hollered.

"I forgot to give you the key. How was I supposed to know you'd take the car anyway? I thought someone stole it. I'll call them right away and clear this thing up."

Florin was a strange cat. Nice guy, but I was beginning to wonder. First, he didn't take off work like everyone else. If you're leaving the country and never coming back, what does it matter if your boss loses a little faith in you? I know my boss was upset with my missing work, but I didn't care. I didn't plan on being there much longer. And, secondly, wouldn't it make more sense to wait until we came back to see if the car you had loaned someone was in their possession before calling the police? Why would you want to bring attention to yourself just before fleeing the country?

On the way back home I expressed my skepticism to Genu.

"Mark, even if he's an informer, which I don't think he is, what can we do about it? Report him? Kick him out of the band? At this point, the best thing we can do is act like he's on board. And if we're forced to do something drastic, he cannot know we suspect anything."

For my own peace of mind, I decided to believe Florin was not an informer, but just a little slow-witted.

- - -

The excitement of leaving was like a fever that got higher as the day of departure came closer. It was all I could think about. It was all we talked about; there was chatter of Porsches and mansions with swimming pools, shelves filled with rock and roll records and beer from every country in the world. But some guys were starting to get a little worried, particularly Lucian. He'd heard his uncle's prison stories and had to try hard to keep his mind far from the realm of possible repercussions.

I was too excited and stubborn to think about what I was getting into. I didn't think about prison and I didn't think about forced labor. I also tried not to think of the possibility that I'd never see my family again.

Dad came over three days before liftoff. He noticed Genu sleeping on my couch.

"Who's that?" he asked.

"That's a friend. He asked if he could stay here for a few days," I answered.

Dad reached into his pocket and handed me an envelope. It was from the Ministry of Defense. It was open.

"What's this?"

"You've been drafted into the army," he said.

"Hmm."

"You *are* going to show up, right?"

"Tăticu, I have better things to do," I said.

"*Better* things to do?" His eyebrows came together. "Mark, you don't mess around with these people. If you don't go, they'll throw you in jail. It's better that you go."

"Better for whom?"

"What's going on Mark? Is your work alright?" he asked.

"Yeah…it's okay."

"Hey, it's what you wanted to do. Things could be much worse."

"Or they could be much better."

"I don't get you," he said, shaking his head.

Dad probably sensed something was off. But I couldn't jeopardize my family and tell him. Even though nothing was certain, the most probable way to keep him from getting in trouble, once I left, was for authorities to be convinced he never knew anything about my leaving.

Before he left, I awkwardly embraced him. "It might be a while before I see you again. Life's getting hectic," I said.

"Welcome to life, son." He patted my shoulder. "You'll figure something out."

- - -

It was the day of. A few more hours and we were off.

Genu, Nick, and I were walking by a popular tea house in Reșița when I noticed an old acquaintance. Johnny was the brother of a former classmate. I had met him several times. He only resembled his sibling by way of his red hair. His brother was a big, brutish boy, whereas Johnny was much the opposite: skinny and fragile-looking. Although he seemed sketchy—he walked somewhat hunched and regularly squinted his right eye, making it seem like he was scoping something out—he wasn't without his charm.

"Johnny, how are you?" I asked.

"Hey Mark! You know…just going here and there," he said, bobbing his head.

"We were just about to go in there." I said and motioned toward the entrance. "These are my friends Nick and Genu."

The boys greeted each other with head nods. I asked Johnny to join us for "tea." Everyone knew that if you wanted booze, you could get it at the tea house. You simply informed the barista how much "extra sugar" you wanted in your tea.

We sat at a round table by the window. I sipped my beverage and asked Johnny about his life. He summed it up as being one big game of cards. The sole source of his income came from gambling. Lately he'd been on a losing streak and was a little perturbed. I couldn't tell if that was the reason for his distraction, or if there was more to it than he was letting on. He continually looked out the corner of his eye when talking. And his face sporadically changed moods for split seconds, as if he thought he saw the grim reaper walk through the door.

Johnny was an animated fellow. His face contorted in correlation with the nature of what he was expressing. His arms flailed, swiped and cut through as though he was directing a confused orchestra. And therein lay his charisma, the same attribute which may have prompted me to present him with an opportunity I would have wanted, had I been in his place.

"Hey…" I waited for him to put his arm down. "We're going to the other side of the fence," I whispered.

He stopped and fixed his eyes on mine.

"You want to come?" I asked.

His face was as straight as I'd ever seen it. I couldn't tell if he was confused, intrigued, excited or numb.

"When?" he asked.

"Tonight. We leave for Timişoara," Genu cut in.

All eyes were on Johnny. It was hard to tell what was going through his head. Maybe the police were on his tail and that was occupying his thoughts. Maybe it was the debts he owed. Or perhaps he was like some of us and thinking of sports cars, women and records. What I did know was that the 23-year-old gambler took precisely 14 seconds to make a decision, which would most certainly change the course of his life forever.

"I'll go," he said.

The band was assembled. We were off for the first leg of our mission. We boarded the train to Timişoara.

-4-
ON THE RUN

"Papers, people! Have your papers ready!"

The unshaven man in the green military uniform had a formidable rifle secured to his back. I didn't want to find out how fast he could transfer it to the other side of his body.

We watched as a sizable crowd gathered on the platform. Then we squirreled our way into the middle of the herd as the train screeched to a halt. An old man wearing a ragged sheepskin ushanka hat muttered under his breath about the loss of respect among the youth.

By the time Genu handed his I.D. papers to the serious man with the shiny boots and the big firearm, there was little time for the man to consult his MOST WANTED list. The herd was getting impatient. He inspected Genu's papers no closer than mine. *Picture looks like him. Expiration date well into the future. Alright, move on. Next.*

Although we had a backup plan, it wasn't one we wanted to implement: Genu would run and try to avoid getting shot or caught, while the rest of us would pretend we didn't know the guy, board the train and hope to meet him at the rendezvous spot.

The plan was to use public transportation only until the small border town of Ciacova. From Ciacova we were going to walk out of Romania, at least a good 20-mile walk.

The train to Timișoara chugged by a landscape I might never see again. Despite the barren winter trees and faded grass, it was still magnificent countryside. In the summer, the landscape would look like the backdrop to a scene from *The Sound of Music*, complete with smooth rolling hills, vibrant grass and chirping birds in every fruit tree.

Every once in a while, off in the distance I saw a villager leading a cow, or a horse-drawn carriage making its way through the country-side. This is my country, I thought. These are my people. Why are we so different? How can they be content with this?

- - -

I told the front desk clerk in the hotel I wanted the biggest single room he had. "I have work to do. I may have some colleagues join me."

"What kind of work do you do?"

"I'm an electrician," I blurted out.

"Will you be meeting other electricians?" he asked.

"Other electrical engineers," I said, hoping to convince the man.

"Oh." The middle-aged man slyly nodded in a way I interpreted to mean he would be fine with hearing no more about me, or whichever of my titles I claimed. He only asked because it was part of his job.

He wrote something down, rummaged through a deep drawer filled with keys and various trinkets, and upon triumphantly finding it, handed me a small gold-plated key with a white tag attached by a thin string.

"Room 704," the clerk said, eyes on his notepad. "Name?"

I hesitated. "Ho…Hobafcovich."

He tilted his head up and slightly squinted. He put his hand out. I searched my pocket, pulled out a wad of *lei* notes and counted out his share.

"Room 704," he said again.

The biggest room available was not nearly big enough, all things considering. Four of us would share the two beds and the rest would sleep on the floor. But for the time being, the floor was occupied by a large map of Romania, several cups acting as ashtrays, and seven bodies laid out at various angles, all facing the center of attention: the map.

We reiterated what we'd already established. Then we dove into newer details.

"I think we should split up until we get to Ciacova." Nick took a puff from his Kent cigarette.

"Absolutely. Some of us could take the bus and others a taxi," Genu added.

"Lucian will come with me. I want to take the bus," Nick added.

"Me and Mark can come with you guys," Johnny said.

"I'm okay with that," Genu said. "It's probably better I stay out of sight the closer we get to my old post anyway."

"I guess we'll go with you then," Florin said to Genu, pointing to Boots. Boots nodded.

"Another thing, guys," Florin said. "I don't think it's a good idea for all of us to have so much money on us. If we are stopped and searched they probably won't search us all. But if they find thousands of *lei* on any one of us, they'll be suspicious. I think it's better that one person hide all the money on him."

We had a good chunk of change on us, about 20,000 *lei*. The average of a decent monthly earning was 3,000 *lei*.

"Do *you* want to carry the money?" I asked Florin.

Although I was only half-convinced of Florin's logic, I had my own. We were going to hoof miles of back road in the dead of night. I thought he should carry the money because if I was looking for easy prey to rob, I would aim for him last. I would rob Boots first, who, by the way, was planning on hiking miles of railroad track in his flashy, slippery-soled boots, and Florin last.

"They're the only shoes I have," Boots retorted, when I mentioned the problems his footwear might pose. "I'll be fine."

He was a stubborn little guy.

"What about supplies?" I asked. "We need some sort of supplies, no?"

"Whatever we're going to get, it's best we get it here. It'll be dark when we get to Ciacova and there'll be nothing but a bar and a few houses there anyway," Genu said.

"I'll stop by the store tomorrow right after we check out," I said.

"Also guys, we need to pick up a bottle of liquor. It'll be cold. Alcohol will help keep us warm," Johnny suggested.

"You boys let me worry about the liquor," Florin said. "There's a shop owner I deliver to in the Square. We have an understanding." Florin was starting to come out of his shell. He was speaking complete sentences. "But if you can find some meat, get that," he added.

"I don't mean to interrupt, but where are we going to put all this stuff? We don't have any bags," Lucian said.

"We'll carry it on us. It's really not that much," Nick said. "We can't carry bags with food and liquor. It'll slow us down, especially if we have to run."

"Run?" Lucian put his head down.

At the end of the night, Genu insisted we get rid of the map. "Burn it in the sink," he told us.

"Are you sure?" I asked. "You know we only get one shot at this."

"It's all up here." He tapped his head. "If we're searched on the way to Ciacova and the map is found, we're in big trouble."

The map was burned in the bathroom sink. Johnny used its flames to light his last cigarette before turning in.

- - -

"You boys got the last one. All that's left until next week are patriots."

The pudgy grocer with the thick mustache sold us his last ham. He smelled like he may have rolled in it before selling it.

"Can you cut it up?" I asked him.

"You know why they call pigs' feet patriots?" he shouted while chopping into the ham.

"Because they're the only things to never leave Romania." Nick had heard that one before.

"Ha, ha! Right you are. Because they're the only ones to never leave Romania!"

He wrapped the bundles of ham in four separate paper bags and wiped his hands with a dirty rag. "Anything else?"

"Three packs of Snagovs," I said.

"So, where are you boys going?" he asked, scanning the wall of cigarette packs.

"We're going to visit family," Nick said.

"You two are related?" the mustached man asked.

"Cousins."

"Second...cousins," Nick said.

"My side of the family got the looks," I said.

"Ha ha!" He placed the packs of cigarettes on the counter and put his hands on his hips. "Well boys, 52 *lei* and you can be on your way."

I paid and wished the jolly grocer a good day.

"That old man sure took his time. We need to hurry up," Nick said, looking at his watch.

We jogged through Opera Square, doing our best to avoid bumping into anyone. We saw the bus pulling up in the distance. Johnny and Lucian were standing in the waiting area and looking back, perhaps a bit worried we might not make it in time.

"What took you guys so long?" Lucian asked.

"The grocer needed a friend," Nick said.

The bus hissed as it slowed to a stop, and the rusty folding doors screeched open.

"What's in the bag?" Johnny asked.

"*Mușchi țigănesc,*" I said.

"Did you get a bottle of French wine to go with it?" Johnny asked.

"It was the last one—"

"Johnny, stop talking and move!" Nick said.

"Yes, sir! I'm excited about this ham, that's all."

"Yeah, yeah. Just watch your step and have your papers ready."

- - -

Except for the occasional person meandering around the bar by the bus station platform, I saw few signs of life as I stepped off the bus in Ciacova. A patron walked out of the bar and John Lee Hooker's scraggly voice could be heard playing through the open door: *"Boom, boom, boom, boom/ Gonna shoot 'ya right down/right off 'yur feet."*

It was six o'clock and already dark.

"Where are they?" Lucian asked, scanning the platform.

"They're probably around the back," Nick said. "It wouldn't be very smart to wait here."

We found Genu, Florin and Boots huddled together —feet together, hands in one pocket, and the other one holding a cigarette—behind the bar. The railroad tracks were just yards away beyond a barren ravine.

"How long have you guys been here?" I asked.

"Long enough to have a drink in the bar," Boots said.

"You didn't?" Nick's expression was piercing.

"He's just kidding. Calm down." Florin patted Nick on the shoulder. "So, what did you guys get?"

"We're in good shape. We got the last of the ham and plenty of cigarettes," I said.

"Great. Florin managed to get a bottle of cognac," Boots said.

Florin pulled the glass bottle out of his pocket, brandishing it like a trophy. It wasn't full.

"What? We've been sitting in the cold," he said through a lopsided smile.

"Well, come on now. Pass it around. I'm getting cold too," Johnny said.

"We need to get going." Genu took his hands out of his pockets. "Let's gather up the money so Florin can hide it in the lining of his jacket. Mark, pass out the ham. We'll need energy for the long walk. Everyone stop playing around."

Lucian was already facing the tracks. He was staring at them as though confronting an old arch nemesis.

The moment I'd been thinking of since I was a kid in Bozovici was here. I was about to embark on the riskiest adventure of my 20 years. The guys I was with I'd known only for a short time. But they would have to be my brothers on this monumental journey. My excitement was two-fold. My hope for the future was only tainted by the realization that the darkest hour was usually right before the sun came up.

I literally left Romania with only the clothes on my back and pockets filled with ham and cigarettes. None of us carried a sack or bag of any sort. Out of seven of us, it never occurred to any of us to bring water. We thought of liquor and cigarettes, but no water. We didn't wear anything different than what we would on any other cold day: tennis shoes, jeans, gloves and our warmest jackets...which would soon prove inadequate.

- - -

Not too long after carefully descending down the ravine and beginning our trek on the tracks, we realized it was going to be a cold and wet night. A subtle yet persistent sleet was coming down, and the temperature was below freezing. It could've been worse. We were surrounded by thin woods on both sides, which slightly diminished the consequence of the wind. I heard branches snap as the wind whistled through the trees.

At some point, maybe an hour into our journey, I felt the ties under my feet vibrating. I stopped walking.

"What's wrong?" Nick asked.

"Nobody feels that?" I said aloud.

Genu, who was in front, stopped.

"I feel it," Lucian said.

"Is that what I think it is?" Genu had turned around.

As we were discussing the source of the vibrating track, we suddenly saw a light quickly chugging its way toward us. The wind was so loud that it managed to drown out the sound of the oncoming train until it was just yards away.

Genu yelled "Off the tracks!" and we all dove onto the shoulder like action movie stars.

"How did we miss that?" Genu asked incredulously.

We lay scattered on the same sunken shoulder like stricken bowling balls. I felt around in my pockets to make sure my ham and cigarettes were still intact. Then I looked around, trying to locate everyone.

Nick said, "That train was probably coming from Toager. Do you think the engineer saw us?"

I didn't want to think about that. Johnny said it made little sense to think about such a possibility. It's not as if we were going to turn back on the slight chance that the engineer might have seen us.

"Hey, keep it down!" Florin said. "There are houses behind these trees. I'm sure there's a nice reward for anyone who reports us."

Just then, the bark from what I presume a bear would sound like, should bears bark, reverberated above the whistling wind. It gave me chills.

Dogs in Romania had a life very different from dogs in the West. For one, if you were a dog in Romania at the time, you came nowhere near the home. You slept, ate and died outside—sun, rain, snow or shine. Secondly, if you were a dog in Romania and you happened to get sick, run over or hit in the head with the neighbor's shovel, there was no doctor that could see you or law to protect you. And since a dog in Romania had most likely never seen a veterinarian, his chances of having rabies were very real. Growing up, I'd been bitten by stray dogs, but I never contracted rabies. And I didn't want to start now. I really wished the dog I was hearing was restrained by a nice, thick, rusty chain – the kind normally used to tie down logs as tall as buildings.

A shadow man, probably heeding the warning roar of his bear-dog, came out of his house to see what the commotion was about. The man grabbed a long stick he kept by the door and then looked around. He slowly walked in our direction and surveyed, with the aid of a lantern, the landscape between his backyard and the tracks. He was some distance off, but still close enough to see us should we become careless and move.

Florin motioned for everyone to get down as he led by example, hitting the ground faster than I had ever seen the big man move. We all followed suit just as the light of the lantern shone in our direction. My head was toward the tracks when I dropped to the ground. I had to turn my neck back to see how close the man was getting. If things were to get dicey, I was going to make sure that I, for one, was not going to get caught.

Fortunately, the villager had no ambition of going beyond the bushes at the edge of his yard. He turned around, cursed at the dog, put the stick back in its place, and slammed the door shut.

The moment the door sealed shut we were already scrambling to our feet and back onto the tracks.

Genu led the way, I followed, Lucian trailed me, and Nick, Johnny, Florin and Boots brought up the rear. Walking the railroad tracks was hard. The distance between the rail ties was two-thirds of a full step. It was like walking with the brakes on.

Aside from someone asking the one with the bottle of cognac to pass it, there was little talking. There was certainly no lighthearted banter. Every crackling twig and snapping branch, every high-pitched whistle, every hint of man-made light startled one of us, if not all. Someone would inevitably stop and ask to help identify the source of the sound. Not only did we have trains and dogs to worry about, but we were getting closer to Toager, which meant we were getting closer to the border post. It was starting to dawn on us just how risky our ambitions really were.

Genu suddenly stopped. "Shhh," he whispered. Though his back was facing us, I could tell he had raised his index finger to his lips.

We looked around. Nick started crouching. By the time Genu turned around, we were all low to the ground. He pointed in the direction of the woods. We duck-walked into the bushes and trees.

"What's happening?" Johnny whispered.

"I heard some talking up ahead," Genu answered.

"Are you sure? Did anyone else hear any talking?" Nick asked.

"I didn't hear anything," Johnny said.

"Me neither," Lucian added.

We looked at each other.

"Well, I heard it," Genu reiterated. "Keep quiet."

"I don't know about this anymore," I heard Boots say. "We've been going for hours. Do we even know where we are?"

"I know where we are!" Genu said, not looking in his direction.

The moon was shining through the trees and right into Boots' eyes. They hardly blinked. He was shivering. I didn't know if he was especially vulnerable to the cold or if he was trembling with fear.

"If we turn back now, we can still be alright," Florin said.

"You think so?" Lucian asked.

"No!" Nick almost broke his whisper tone. "We are already near the border. We have to be. Stop talking like that. Besides, I don't think there is anyone out there." He turned to Genu.

"Maybe not...but I'm sure I heard someone talking. Let's wait a few more minutes before going again."

Nick was the first to step out of from behind the bush and crawl up the shoulder. I looked behind me. There was no telling where someone would pop out of. When I turned my head back around, Nick had already stood up.

"Alright. Let's go," Genu said.

- - -

"Where now, Genu?"

Seven hours after leaving Ciacova we had arrived at the end of the railroad, sore legs and all. The last rail tie was much like the other ones, except that it had no others on its western side. Somewhere under the blanket of pitch black was a little hamlet called Toager. It was one o'clock in the morning. People in places like Toager are not awake at one o'clock in the morning. They don't leave lights on at the entrance door and they don't have street lamps to guide night owls. They don't have night owls. However close Toager may have been, it had no intention of making itself known to us.

"Genu, which way now?" someone asked again.

We'd been standing and looking around for minutes. Around us the land was barren and open, what could be seen of it anyway. There was no path, dirt or paved, no iconic structure—no sign of any kind to aid our disoriented minds. Genu was supposed to be our path, our map. But it seemed he had become a blank page, as good as ashes in a sink.

"I don't know guys. Let me think. Everything looks the same." He looked around confusingly, straining for evidence of something familiar. The drizzling sleet was beginning to take its toll, adding to the misery of the blistering wind. We needed shelter.

"Maybe, if we can ever find the village, someone will take us in for the night," Boots suggested, shivering as he spoke. "I have to sit down. My feet are killing me."

"Why don't we just blow a trumpet and announce to everyone we're here instead?" Genu said. "Have patience. I'll figure out where we are."

Nick came up to me. "If he doesn't figure out where we are, we're going to have to start moving…somewhere." He looked over his shoulder toward Genu.

"You may be right. We can't stay here much longer," I said as I shivered involuntarily and wiped sleet out of my hair.

I walked over to Genu, who was now at the edge of a clearing in the direction we came from. "What do you think?" I asked.

He turned around. His eyes looked worn. "Mark, I really don't know. And I don't know why. I had a clear picture in my head…of everything here. But now, now I can't figure it out." I looked back and could see the rest of the guys huddled together, talking. I went to them.

"Look over there," Johnny said, pointing.

I strained my eyes. "What is that?"

"I don't know. But let's find out. It looks like it might be a house."

"Are you guys serious?" Nick cut in.

"Listen!" Johnny said. "We're not going to knock on the door."

"We're not?" Lucian asked.

"No. Maybe there's a shed or barn behind it. We're in the country, remember? We *need* to get out of this weather. We have to try something."

We followed Johnny. Genu was last, looking back.

We soon realized we weren't going toward a house. It was a barn! Even better. That's when the lightbulb above Genu's head came on. "Guys, I know where we are!" he exclaimed. "That's the barn—that's where the soldiers keep their horses in the summer!"

"Are you sure?" I asked.

"Positive!"

"Why only in the summer?" Johnny asked.

"I don't know," he answered.

"But this is where you were posted, right?" Johnny persisted.

"Yeah...."

"Nobody ever told you why they only keep horses here in the summer?"

"I never asked," Genu said.

"You weren't curious at all?" Johnny asked.

"No! Where are you going with this?"

"What if the barn is some sort of trap? I mean, where else could they keep the horses? They still have horses in the winter, right? Is there another barn somewhere else around the post?" Johnny asked.

"I'm not sure…"

"Guys!" While Genu and Johnny were going back and forth, I had already opened the side entrance door to the barn and had one foot in. I told the guys to shut up and come in. I slowly made another step in and peered around. So far so good. I looked back and told the guys to get in before we froze to death. "Who cares why they don't keep horses here in winter," I added.

I cupped my hands around the delicate flame of my lighter to inspect the barn. The bulky, wooden door creaked as the guys slipped past it. I was able to make out six empty horse stalls and much of nothing else; no hay, no tools, no straps or saddles. It didn't even smell much like a barn. If smelled of wintry pine. More wintry than pine. All clues pointed to an abandoned barn.

"Now what?" Lucian asked.

"First off, keep the lighters to a minimum. I don't know how many lighters it takes for the guys in the watchtowers to see us and I don't want to find out." Genu seemed himself again. "Everyone look around. There should be an opening leading to the loft. We can't stay down here. If someone comes in, we have zero chance of escaping. In the loft, we have *some* chance."

"Why would someone come here?" Lucian asked. "You said it's abandoned."

"The post is right there." Genu pointed beyond the opposite wall of the barn. "You'll see it when daylight comes. Soldiers sometimes use this little road when they come to, or leave from the post." He paused. "Did anyone find the opening?"

We tilted our heads upwards. Genu was right. Toward the southern wall there was a large man-hole type opening about eight feet off the dusty floor.

Everyone thought it would be a good idea to help Florin up first. He was the last person I wanted to pull up. Two of us clasped our hands together as he placed one foot onto each hand, while someone else held him up by his ankles. We lifted and as soon as he was in reach, he pulled himself through the opening. Boots was the last one through.

The roof of the barn was made of terracotta shingles. There was enough space in between to make the wind coming through feel like cleavers made of frost, mercilessly slicing and dicing us with its iced edges.

We huddled close together in a circle, hoping to lessen nature's assault. When we realized we were no warmer than before, we decided to sit behind one another and rub each other's backs. Maybe the friction would warm us up. Then we frisked ourselves; up and down, side to side, on our arms and sides. We were still very cold. I heard Lucian's teeth clattering.

"We need a fire." Florin had been suggesting a fire since we closed the barn door.

"I know, I know. But you guys don't realize how close they are. Right across that field." Genu pointed. "They are standing watch with binoculars and dogs...and AK-47s."

We tried to settle in. We drank the last of the cognac and finished the ham. Someone said eating would warm us up.

It didn't work. We were still cold.

"If we don't make a fire we're going to freeze to death." Florin's tone was almost intimidating by this point. Boots was nodding in agreement. I, for one, couldn't help but begin to agree. "I think he's right. If we don't get caught trying to cross over, we'll be found as ice blocks."

Florin had already begun ripping loose planks off the floor and walls. Nick was gathering loose straw and small sticks. The rest of us followed their example. We reconvened on the eastern-most part of the loft and dumped our findings.

We may have violated one of the first survival rules by forgetting to bring water, but no one in the group was a stranger to making a fire. We first made a small mound using the straw. I then lit the straw with my lighter. As the flame grew, we put small pieces of kindling over it. Once the kindling caught and started popping, we stacked the larger pieces of wood in tepee-fashion.

"Isn't the floor going to catch on fire?" Lucian asked.

"Nah. There's enough dried mud in between these planks and everywhere else on this floor to keep that from happening," Florin told him.

The flame brought the loft to life. Our shadows grew and soon adorned the walls, as the subtlest move was amplified. Every nook and cranny was illuminated. We got the heat we craved, but I hadn't felt as vulnerable since the trip began. It would take an act of God for someone to look across the field and fail to notice the amber glow seeping through the terracotta shingles. All thoughts of exotic cars and mansions were far from our minds. Our dreams now were less glamorous: don't get caught and make it out alive.

One of the guys concluded that we needed a miracle and asked me to pray. Everyone was in agreement. *We need a miracle. Mark, will you ask God for a miracle? I hear He specializes in such things.*

"Why me?" I asked.

"Because your dad is a pastor," Johnny said. "You have the connection. And besides, I'm not even sure God exists. He definitely wouldn't listen to me...."

"I'm not sure it works that way," I said.

Throughout the last few years, I still prayed every once in a while. It was usually out of guilt or fear. Now it would be the latter.

"I'll give it a shot," I said.

Everyone bowed their heads and waited. I prayed something about how scared we were and how capable He was of protecting us. I asked God to get us out of "this mess" safely...and free. I may have even tried striking a deal, saying something about how we'll be good boys if He helps us. Then I said, "Amen." The guys repeated after me. *Amen.*

I'm sure it was a sorry prayer. But I think it helped. Before we knew it, we had almost forgotten about the cold, no doubt aided by the warmth of the miniature fire. Now we were comfortable enough to listen to Genu explain why border soldiers were just as scared of us as we were of them. "They've been sabotaged, stabbed and even shot. That's why some of them, when out in the field, make themselves known: to warn anyone who's there. It's their way of saying, 'Go around.' It's also the reason they don't take any more chances—the fear, that is. If they spot anything that might resemble a human being in the border zone, they'll shoot on the spot. Soldiers have unloaded entire clips at moving bushes," Genu explained.

"Did *you* ever shoot anyone?" Lucian asked.

Genu dropped his head.

"I was stationed here for three months," he began. "I was miserable. The nights were long and cold and the days more of the same. There wasn't much to keep us busy. For some guys, catching someone trying to cross over became a game. The most tempting part about catching someone was the reward. You could get permission to go home for a week; home-cooked meals, time with family and friends, seeing your girlfriend; all good reasons to try and get home.

"Soldiers talked about shooting defectors, but I was never sure if I could believe them. One of the guys was said to have shot someone in the head. But he never talked about it and I didn't really want to ask him." He sighed. "I'm kind of glad I never got my vacation."

It was well-known that most soldiers stationed on the western border were from the other side of the country. The reason has to do with the reversed L-shaped barrier formed by the Carpathian Mountains through the center of the country. The Western ideas that flowed into the country from avenues such as Radio Free Europe almost completely stopped at the Carpathians. The signal couldn't easily get over the mountains and through to the other side, say to Dobrogea, or down to Oltenia. One of the exceptions to the rule was Constanţa, a port city by the Black Sea. The result of the mountainous wall was an eastern population far less exposed, and consequently, less sympathetic, to Western ideals. It made sense to put someone from say, Moldova, on the western border at Grăniceri; because the eastern Romanian truly believed all things *West* were of the evil empire. He was more likely to perceive those who wanted to leave the motherland as unpatriotic scum looking to join their enemy.

For the most part.

Genu's family was from Ialomiţa, a county sandwiched between Bucharest and the port of Constanţa. His father later moved his family to the other side of the mountains, to Transylvania, for work. Shortly after, Genu caught a case of Western sympathies from friends and Radio Free Europe. Being stationed at Grăniceri years later only further reinforced his desire to live in the West.

"By the time I was stationed here, I never wanted to catch anyone," he said, staring into the fire. "And I never did. Come to think of it, my time at the post may have been the best time to escape. I'm sorry I didn't think about it then." He sighed. "I guess I'd better make this time count."

We awoke at six, still intact and undetected. I can't say I actually slept. I don't think anyone did. I dozed off into the purgatory state of half asleep-half awake, but sleep is not what I would've called it.

Once daylight broke, the fire was put out. There were fewer obvious ways to announce our presence than with a smoke cloud.

Throughout the night we took turns stoking the fire. When we weren't feeding the fire or halfway sleeping, we were busy being startled by every sound that stood out. Our paranoia was not completely unwarranted.

Barely an hour after the smoke had cleared, we were brought to fully-awake status by the muffled plodding of hoofs into dirt. The sound was nearing. We rushed to peek through the shingles. Making its way down the winding dirt path, which ran parallel to the barn, was a horse-drawn carriage that looked like an oversized open box with missing flaps. At first, we only saw that both passenger seats were occupied. As the two brown horses dragged the cart closer, it became apparent that the passengers, wearing the stereotypical Soviet-style fur hats and green overcoats, were soldiers. The open-box carriage was empty.

We took our eyes off the incoming carriage and looked at each other, perhaps everyone hoping to find a face without panic written all over it. The most frozen of faces were Florin's and Boots'. I could only suspect that Florin may have been having flashbacks of his days in the canals. Boots had the look of a naive kid who just realized the possibility that our mission might lead not to another country, but to the worst this country had to offer. "What do we do if they come in here?" he whispered, looking at Genu.

Genu didn't acknowledge him. He just stared at the incoming carriage. Boots already knew the answer. We all knew the answer.

Nothing.

What *can* you do? On the opposite side of where we entered the barn were two large doors. But it didn't matter. You can't craftily open the doors on one side, sneak through, and close them behind just as the soldiers enter the barn through the other side. We weren't in a movie. This was real life. If soldiers were going to enter the barn, our best plan was to stay put, be quiet, and pray that God extended the answer to the prayer I prayed during the night.

The carriage with the loud jesting soldiers continued to roll toward us. We watched each wheel revolution as if our lives depended on it. For a moment, we started to relax. But before passing the barn, the soldier with the reins suddenly stopped.

"Whoa!" he roared, tugging back the straps.

My heart immediately began to speed up. The soldier looked around, first to his left, then at the barn. We ducked to the floor, forgetting that he couldn't see us.

"Ionel, do you smell that?" the man asked.

Ionel wanted to know what his comrade smelled.

"Smoke," he answered. "Smells like a fire. You don't smell that?"

"I smell a little smoke, but it's probably from your jacket. You smoke like a chimney," Ionel said.

"Nah. Smells like someone has been burning wood."

"Where would someone be a making a fire? I don't see anything."

There was a pause as the man turned his head. "Maybe in the barn."

"Stop fooling around! We have to get back and deliver another round of supplies. Let the guys stationed here worry about it."

"Ya!" the driver yelled. The carriage restarted its forward motion until it rolled out of sight.

- - -

Throughout the day, we noticed a total of six guards in as many watchtowers. They mostly paced back and forth. A couple of the soldiers led large sheepdogs between the towers. All of them were strapped with bulky military-style rifles. They looked bored to tears, talking and smoking, doing what they could to pass the time. Every once in a while – as if having a momentary conviction of duty – a guard scanned the area with his binoculars.

The first thing we noticed was that we would have to cross a small cemetery, which was a few yards in front of the barn. Some of the graves looked open. "They got tired of carrying corpses back to town," Genu explained. "Digging graves is the initiation task of new guards."

Past the cemetery was an open field scattered with large hay bales. Once we made it through the field we would have to cross over a few large holes, or trenches. Genu explained that the trenches were dug so invading tanks would fall in them. Once we navigated over the trenches, we only had the watchtowers to get by. It looked like open field from there. We couldn't see any further.

"Where's the fence we have to climb over?" I asked.

"Not here," Genu answered.

"Where is it then?" Nick asked.

"I don't know. Maybe somewhere past the towers."

"Then where's the border?" Johnny asked.

"I don't know. We were never allowed to go beyond the watchtowers."

We looked at each other. I didn't want to say anything. I once overheard someone talk about how the military sometimes put a fence perpendicular to the way out, as a way to confuse anyone trying to escape. The confused escapee would assume the fence was a barrier to the other side and climb over it, only to fall back in the same country.

We didn't need any more reason for concern.

"One last thing before we go," Genu said. "Watch out for animal traps. They are small and few, but they're out there, and they hurt."

"Guys," I said. "There's no turning back. This is it. If we go back, we have zero chance to gain freedom. If we go forward we at least have one chance." I'm not sure what made me say it, but it seemed to have had the opposite of its intended effect on Florin.

"I don't think I'll be going with you guys," he said.

"What?"

"You came all this way. You avoided getting hit by a train, almost froze to death – now you want to go back?" Nick asked.

Florin sheepishly shrugged his shoulders and nodded.

"Yeah, I think I'm going back with him too," Boots added.

"Do you guys realize how risky it is to go back?" Genu said. "Can you even find the railroad tracks?"

"We'll figure it out," Florin said. "Maybe we'll go through the town."

Genu scoffed and shook his head. "If you talk to anyone, please, *please*, don't mention us."

Maybe watching the soldiers all day was too much for them.

If it weren't for Florin we would've frozen to death. I hated to see him go.

- - -

It was dark. We creaked open the door and slipped out of the barn. Florin and Boots went one way, the rest of us forward.

We split up as we worked our way toward the cemetery. Once in the cemetery, we used the tombstones to conceal us.

We were halfway through when my foot slipped into an open grave. I almost lost my balance and fell in. Relieved to be above ground, I composed myself. A song I'd heard many times as a kid in church came to mind. I wasn't trying to think of anything comforting. I wasn't trying to think at all. But a song so fitting, which I believe only reinforces the idea that what seeps in times of distress is what you're really made of, played in my head. To this day I don't know the name of the song, but the first verse resonated with me more than it ever had when I'd heard it in church:

> *When you are in dire straits*
> *When the ground beneath you is sinking*
> *When you have no one else*
> *Run to Jesus*

Just as we finished crossing the cemetery, we heard a loud noise, a bell of some sorts, perhaps a village alarm, clanging. It was coming from Toager.

I don't know what ever happened to Florin and Boots. I'd heard rumors. I think the bell was probably a precursor to their capture.

Genu and I moved up, a few yards past the cemetery. The others, now down to three —Nick, Lucian and Johnny — stayed at the edge of the cemetery. Before we left, we decided it wasn't a good idea to clump together. A clump was noticeable.

- - -

The watchtowers stood yards away. Beyond them, stood the possibility of a new life and the bridge to a different world, one without tyranny. We needed one last good push.

-5-

ZRENJANIN

The old man turned us in. His wife kept us distracted with coffee, warmth and incomprehensible conversation, while her husband was waving over the police. No wonder she kept talking when she knew we didn't understand her. What a sly old lady.

"How's Romania now?" Iosef asked. I was in the front seat of the compact Yugo. Genu sat in the back, almost taking it up entirely. Nick, Lucian and Johnny were walking with Filip. Every so often I turned around to see if they hadn't run away. The police station was just a few minutes' night stroll down the road, we were told. It was a necessary part of the process. "Don't worry. You'll get where you want to go," we were assured.

"Bad," I answered, my head turning back toward the front. We were certainly not risking health and life to leave a good Romania.

"It seems to get worse every year," Genu added.

"If we are going to get you boys where you want to go, we first have to make a declaration," Iosef said, ignoring what I said about Romania.

Although I'd been in Yugoslavia for a total of only a half an hour, I already noticed a difference. The few words exchanged in the car with Iosef revealed a warmth and lack of antagonistic force from authority very seldom found in the old country, so seldom, in fact, that no one I know had ever experienced it. Iosef carried on as if we were two old acquaintances discussing yesterday's soccer game.

The station was a small one-story building which, by this time, was deserted. Or, for all I know, it could've been at full staff the moment

Iosef and Filip stepped back in the building. We were told to sit down in the entrance room of the building. On the far wall, in front of the window, was a hulking, ancient-looking oak desk. There was a stack of papers in one corner and a white notepad in the center. We were asked to gather some of the scattered chairs and sit down in front of the desk, behind which Iosef had already settled and was on his way to lighting a cigarette with a black Zippo lighter. With a ballpoint pen in his right hand, he was ready to go. With the fuming cigarette now suspended in the corner of his mouth, he first turned to Johnny. "Name?"

"Johnny Bacalli."

Iosef asked Johnny where he was from, his occupation, marital status, and, finally, about his family. "What does each parent do? Where are they now? Tell me about your siblings." Johnny had reservations about revealing certain things. When asked what certain siblings did, he simply said he wasn't in contact with them, something I suspected wasn't true.

Iosef went on with the declarations, asking everyone else the same questions. We answered respectfully, perhaps keeping in mind that we were at the man's mercy. I, for one, was beginning to trust him. There was something in his demeanor I thought genuine. He was persuasive like that.

Iosef's final question was, "Why are you here?" We all answered the same: *Communism is a failed oppressive system and we don't want to live under it anymore.*

Iosef wrote down the last words of the declaration while five pairs of eyes stared at his pen. He was very stoic, as if the political structure we were aching to escape was not the same one he was living under. Yugoslavia was communist too, but I suppose what made it a little different was that it did a better job of appeasing the West. They were known to work with the United Nations and NATO at times. But it was also widely known that Yugoslavia turned back more escapees than they helped defect. We'd heard, long before we fled, that for every person returned back to Romania, Yugoslavia received an exorbitant amount of salt in return, something like a truck-full. Apparently there was a salt shortage in Yugoslavia.

Iosef stood up, put his pen in the slight drawer under the desk top, grabbed the papers he'd been writing on, and lined them up by tapping them on the desk. "Alright boys, let's go."

"That's it?"

"For here it is. We have to print these documents and start the submission process. Now we go to Zrenjanin."

The city of Zrenjanin is named after Žarko Zrenjanin Uča. Uča was a Communist leader sometime during the first half of the 20th century. During World War II, he was imprisoned and tortured by the Nazis. Later on, after he'd been released, he was caught trying to skip town. He was killed shortly afterwards.

On the way to a town named after a guy who was killed for trying to escape, Iosef revealed to us that we were going to a *zatvor*. He mixed Romanian and Serbian words, perhaps hoping to conceal the reality of what a *zatvor* was. "It's part of the process," he kept saying. "You will be there for 20 days."

"Yes, but what is a *zatvor?*" Genu asked.

"It's kind of like a holding cell," Iosef answered.

"Kind of?"

It's part of the process.

We figured out what a *zatvor* was as we rolled up the long driveway leading to the gated tunnel with the armed guard in front of it. Beyond the dark tunnel was a fenced and barbed-wired courtyard that encircled a large three-story building. The tall narrow windows on the grimy walls of the building were barred and, thanks to the barely-sufficient lighting in the courtyard, we saw that the cracked stucco had seen better days. In Romania nothing was well-lit.

Zatvor means prison. The burly and aged guard at the entrance motioned for us to follow him. Iosef and Filip got back in their cars and drove off. Their part in the process was over.

Once inside, we were instructed to put our belongings in a small plastic bag. This took no time at all, as how we had nothing but our I.D.'s. We were led past several cells, some occupied, and up the stairs to the third floor. Burly Guard eventually showed us to our room. It was a large holding cell with 27 beds (I would have plenty of time to count and recount those beds in the upcoming days).

Burly Guard pointed to the room, unlocked the barred door, and asked us to follow him again. He led us to another large room. This room had a discolored tile floor and several shower heads, most of which hung from the ceiling. We were each given a bar of soap and a white bed sheet, which was supposed to also serve as a towel.

We turned the water on, stripped down and showered, each of us under our own streaming surge. The hot torrent now hitting my cold skin was second only to that most glorious cup of coffee I had at the old couple's home. I wanted to revel under its steaming comfort for hours. Never mind I was surrounded by my naked friends. As far as I was concerned, they weren't there. I'm sure they felt the same. No one said anything. For two days I had been in a constant state of cold. The hot shower was the exact measure of heat I'd been craving since I stepped off the bus in Ciacova. Too bad we were rushed.

Since we were not given clothes, we had no choice but to trot back to our cells in our underwear and bed sheets. We used the hot water and remaining soap to clean the mud off our jeans and sweaters as best as possible. The clothes would have to dry overnight by the radiator heater in the room.

Aside from beds and the lone heat dispenser, there was little else in the large holding cell. Four tall windows, accessible only by climbing the heater or the beds, would give us a glimpse of the outside world.

I wrapped myself in one of the available blankets. Someone suggested we make sure the radiator was at full blast. It was. We each claimed a bed in the right corner of the large room.

No sooner had we lain down, partially mummified, that we were interrupted by a guard carrying a large tray. We stared at him with wide eyes and gawking mouths. *Is that what we think it is?* We didn't think to offer to help him. We didn't flinch. If we were going to help this man carry the tray, he probably wouldn't have survived.

The tray supported one large loaf of the whitest bread I'd ever seen, a roll of liverwurst spread, and a large tin pitcher of water. There was a single knife for cutting and for spreading, and a brown clay cup.

We voraciously devoured everything on that tray. The bread was soft, the *pâté* perfect, and the water just a tad too cold.

The lights were turned off very shortly after the last of the food was gone. A different guard walked to the door. He clapped his hands and zipped his right hand across his closed mouth. It was bedtime, we understood. But before the guard walked away, Johnny walked to the door to tell the man he needed to go to the bathroom. *"Toaleta?"* he said.

The guard smirked.

Johnny, thinking the guard did not understand, made it look like he was urinating on the ground. *"Toaleta!"* he repeated.

The guard pointed to the left side of the room and grinned again. *"Kabla,"* he retorted.

"Johnny, I think he's pointing to the bucket," I suggested.

On the opposite side of the room, in the corner, was a rusty bucket that looked like it had been salvaged from a burning building.

"Are you serious?" I suppose even Johnny had his standards.

The guard walked away. *Kabla.*

The bathroom was not in the room. And there was no one to walk you to the bathroom at night. The bucket was your only option. It was emptied once a day. And even during the day, you only got one visit to the conventional toilet. Strategy was highly advised. *Plan your visit carefully.*

As for me, I was too tired to brood over having to use the filthy bucket.

For the most part, things were looking good. A constant source of heat was filling the air, I had food in my belly and the hope of living in a free land was alive and well. That was enough for me. At this time yesterday, we were walking half-steps on rail tracks against a vicious wind. We were fearfully sneaking past dormant towns like Ghilad and Banloc, towns occupied by people who probably never dreamed of risking their lives for something as unsure and ambiguous as the dream of living free; a dream whose most tangible attribute was a vague desire to *just be free.* The people in those sleepy towns probably never had a dream propelled by the uncertain hope that even a simple man without great strategy, adequate resources and extensive training, can cross the planet, in spite of trained resistance, and end up where he wishes to (even though he is not entirely sure where that place is) and live a fulfilling life. Twelve hours later, we had miraculously survived a nerve-wracking night by huddling together as we tried to ease the blows of the Balkan weather. Then I asked the only God I knew of to block the amber glow of the fire that kept us alive from the sight of our potential executioners. It seemed this is exactly what happened: God blinded our enemies.

Kabla or no *kabla*, things were looking good. Phase one of Operation Freedom had been completed. I was going to sleep.

- - -

The sun had barely peeked through when I was rudely awakened by obnoxious yelling. The voice belonged to a backward individual with a deep voice. The red-headed, big-boned guard rattled the cell bars with his club while he yelled in Serbian. His face was as flush as his hair. His eyes stammered wide open. The veins in his forehead were attempting escape. And his teeth ground in between syllables and the release of spittle sprinkles.

I'm not exactly sure how we learned it, but the insane morning guard we would grow to loathe was ethnically Hungarian. Although he wouldn't dare sink so low as to utter a single Romanian word, it was obvious he hated Romanians. We didn't understand most of what he was saying, but we were certain he was cursing at us, among other things.

"Ceaușescu!" he roared. He pointed, then panoramically wiped his bulging, pale arm across his body in an attempt to communicate to my friends and I that we were going back. He made a slitting gesture across his throat. "Ceaușescu!" he bellowed again, followed by pointing in our direction. He walked away, laughing like a maniacal villain in a fairy tale.

The guard's animosity may have been a result of the tumultuous history between Hungary and Romania. Or maybe it was simpler than that: perhaps the guy was just plain crazy.

Crazy Guard did not prevent another guard, a saner one, from bringing us the tea, salami, and bread and butter that comprised our breakfast. The same guard brought lunch, some kind of potato stew with chunks of mystery meat, and, again, bread and water. Lunch was served with an extra side of terror as Crazy Guard came behind

Silent Guard and yelled almost the entire time we were eating. Dinner, we'd learn, was consistently better than other meals. This first day, it consisted of some kind of cooked pork trimmings with a side of bread and water.

Day One was almost over.

"Guys, this has been one of the most boring and longest days of my life," Lucian said. "Do you really think we'll have to be here for 20 days?"

"I don't see why not," Nick answered.

"I hope that maniac won't act like that every day. Even in the army, I hated it when people yelled at me," Genu said, finishing the last of his bite.

"He yelled at all of us…he hates us all, if it makes you feel any better," I said.

"It doesn't."

"I need a cigarette." Johnny had his own troubles.

"I don't think they care. You made it pretty obvious. They just looked at you funny. You should be happy you're getting food," Nick said.

"I am. I want to be happier. A cigarette will make that happen."

There was little to keep us occupied in that big cell. The only newspapers were outdated Serbian ones, and no one thought to bring us magazines or books.

Our nerves were wearing thin. On top of the boredom, there was the fear of the unknown, cabin fever and the consistent harassment of the crazy freckled guard grinding us down. Genu's concern was warranted. Crazy Guard harassed us every day since our first. It wouldn't take long for things to come to a boil.

We were about a week into our stay when Crazy Guard stopped by for his daily lunch harassment routine. We hadn't seen him in the morning. He may have felt there was some abuse to make up. He was going through his usual cursing, spitting and teeth-grinding routine with an extra dose of rancor this afternoon. At one point he stomped his feet and slapped the bars.

"I think he's drunk," Nick said.

Genu, who'd been irritated all morning, yelled back at him, power-walked to the bars and pointed his finger at the man. "You're just a fat, ugly, backwards fool," he started. "I'm tired of listening to you! Every day you come in here and make a fuss! Shut up! Shut —"

Crazy Guard opened the cell door so fast that Genu couldn't even finish his rant before being interrupted by the man's fist and, consequently, the hard cell floor. I watched in astonishment as the guard, like a satisfied hyena, turned his attention to us while standing over Genu. We stood by the edge of our beds with partially chewed food in our gaping mouths.

We had discussed a strategy should the man ever leave us little choice but to defend ourselves. We sure had plenty of time. The plan was rather simple. There were five of us. The man had four limbs and one head. Nick and I would lunge at his feet and, hopefully, take the bear down. Johnny and Lucian will grab his arms and hold him down, while Genu will be in charge of attacking his face or torso. He was the heavyweight. What we never discussed was a backup plan, should we be one man down. Right now, it didn't look like Genu was in any position to be the point man. He was on the floor, rubbing his face, maybe making sure everything was still there.

Fortunately, we didn't have to improvise. I guess the guard quenched his violent thirst when he laid Genu out. He stepped over Genu as he turned around, casually walked through the cell door, locked it, and walked away as if nothing happened. I'm pretty sure I saw an extended grin peeking from the side of his face.

"Genu, what did you do that for?" Nick asked.

"I couldn't stand it anymore!" He was standing up. "The guy is psychotic!"

"Of course he is! But we still have two weeks to go. What if you ruined your chance – *our chances* – of getting to the other side?" Nick stood up.

"Who knows if they'll even let us go. They're probably lying to us. It's not like they're much different here. All these Communists are the same. They're all—"

"Right, Genu. So ruin any chance we may have because you cannot control yourself and—"

"Guys!" I shouted. "Stop it! It happened. It's over now. If they were going to let us go, I'm sure this incident didn't change anything. How much pull can that maniac have? Let's just relax. Nothing good is going to come from arguing."

Most of the anxiety came from the fact that no one told us anything. Sure, we were told we'd have to spend 20 days in the *zatvor*, but Iosef never told us what exactly was to come after those 20 days. Yes, it was part of the process, but what else was part of the process? Here at Zrenjanin, no one ever updated us, or reassured us that everything was still on track. Not one person since we'd been here spoke a word we understood.

We were in no way, shape or form at ease about the prospect of being released in the West. Whatever spark of hope we had that first night had dwindled down to a miserable, dying ember. We begin to talk more about the stories we had heard of people who were turned back, and less of what the other side may be like. It didn't help that we weren't allowed outside until a week after our stay began. Cabin fever hit us hard. Being stuck in a room with the same group of guys for days without having anything constructive to do was a special kind of torture.

- - -

I knew what day it was when I awoke. We all knew. We'd been tallying the days. We made it to day 20 without any more incidents.

We had breakfast at its usual time. No one said anything. Just another breakfast. "Maybe they'll come and talk to us as we're eating," one of the guys suggested.

Maybe.

Nine o'clock rolled around, or thereabouts, and still nothing.

"They don't even know it's day 20, do they?" Genu said. "Here we are counting the days off like fools, and to them it's just another Thursday."

"Nah, they know," I said. *I hope they know.*

All morning we hushed at the sound of every step we heard in the distance, listening with anticipatory unease. We homed in on the steps as if we were code breakers, trying to decipher as soon as the first two steps were made whether they were furthering or nearing steps. Many steps teased us. They introduced themselves and just as quickly walked out of our lives.

It may have been around 10 o'clock when a series of taps we'd been zeroing in on went beyond the introduction phase. They were nearing steps. They weren't the normal heavy, thud-like ones of the guards. They sounded more like the tapping of dress shoes.

The worn leather shoes belonged to a portly man named George. George was holding a tattered black briefcase that matched his shoes.

"Well boys, it's the last day, huh?" He smiled wide under a thick, black mustache.

The sound of our native tongue from someone on the other side of the bars never sounded sweeter. We ran up to the bars as if only the first one there would be allowed to leave.

"Are we getting out?" Genu asked.

"*Da.*"

"When?"

"Today," he answered. "Kind of...."

"You're not lying to us, are you?" Genu asked.

"What do you mean 'kind of?'" I asked.

"Boys, the reason you were in here is because you crossed over into Yugoslavia without passports. You had to serve your sentence before you could go on to the next step. From here on out, you will be processed and then allowed to go wherever you want."

Then the man walked away.

We slowly walked back to our corner.

"I don't know if I believe him," Lucian said.

"What did he mean 'kind of?'" I asked. "We're either getting out or not. Right?"

We didn't believe him. Twenty days will do that to you.

It wasn't too long before we heard the tapping of another pair of fancy shoes. This man also stopped in front of our cell. He stood tall in his dark navy blue suit. He supported a stack of papers under one arm, and a ring of keys in his right hand. He looked us over.

"Ho...baf...covich?" he said, eyes on his papers, then into the cell.

I raised my hand. "*Da.*"

Then he called out my friends' names. They raised their hands too.

He opened the door, hooked his finger and motioned for us to follow him. We trailed him down the hall and passed many cells, descended two flights of stairs, and eventually stepped into what I presumed was his office, which happened to be near the entrance we had come through a long 20 days ago.

Two leather chairs faced the desk. I hesitantly took one and Genu the other. The suited man looked at me and began speaking in Serbian. Although I tried to familiarize myself with the language over the last few days, I didn't understand anything the man was saying. I assumed he was addressing me because of my last name. Once he stopped talking, I nodded my head and shrugged my shoulders. *I have no idea what you just said.* He turned his hands over as if to say, *no matter,* and then shot out of his seat.

Follow me.

We were given back the I.D.'s from the plastic bags. We were escorted to the courtyard, where a long black van awaited us. The doors were shut behind us after we sat on the benches screwed to the van walls. We heard the front doors slam shut. The engine was started and we started moving.

"They're taking us back," Johnny pouted.

I sat hunched over, resting my elbows on my knees and staring at the vibrating metal floor. "Maybe not. Maybe they really are going to let us go," I said, keeping my head down.

"I knew we should have run when those two guys came to the old man's house," Johnny said.

"And go where?" Nick asked.

"We had no money; we were tired, hungry and cold. We would've died of hypothermia if we hadn't gotten out of those clothes," I reasoned.

We sat in silence as the diesel van ticked along. At some point, I noticed something peculiar. The van was getting faster. Not only were we picking up speed, but I was hearing large vehicles whooshing and roaring by. They sounded like large trucks. It seemed the road was getting wider, something *very* unlike Romania.

"Maybe we *are* going to Belgrade," Nick said in response to my observation. "Listen to all the commotion" – his eyes rolled up – "we are definitely not in Romania."

"Now that I think about it, I do remember the guy behind the desk mentioning Belgrade," I said.

The more we rode, the more the traffic increased. The roads toward Romania wouldn't be getting wider, we concluded. There were no large highways in Romania, none that we'd ever seen and been on, anyway. Things were sounding good.

The van suddenly stopped. The back doors swung open and one of the men mumbled something as he tried to light a cigarette. He failed twice, but eventually outsmarted the wind (he turned his back to it) and lit his cigarette. He pointed to a little store beyond the parking lot as he handed the lighter to his comrade. He looked at us, pointed to himself and his partner, swung his index finger and then nodded.

"I think we can get out," I said.

We stepped out of the van and watched the men walk away and into a coffee shop about 50 yards beyond.

"I wonder if they're going to bring us back coffee," Lucian said.

"Never mind the coffee. What is going on?" Genu asked.

"We must be going to Belgrade," Nick said.

"I want a cigarette. I should've asked them for one." Johnny stubbed his heel on the ground.

"Look, guys. There's no way they would leave us out like this if they were planning on returning us," I said.

"Mark, you said it yourself. There's no way for us to make it here on our own. What are they afraid we'll do if we run off? We don't speak a word of Serbian, we have no money and no passports." Genu said. "Maybe this 'easygoing gimmick' they're playing is part of a strategy to make their jobs easier. You know, 'Let's pretend there's nothing to worry about and they'll behave right up until we no longer need them to.'"

"Still guys, I have a good feeling about this." And I did.

The two men came back with coffee in their hands and were smoking freshly lit cigarettes. They shooed us back into the van, slammed the doors shut and off we went again.

The van didn't stop until we arrived in Padinska Skela, a settlement outside of Belgrade. More importantly, we arrived in the Padinska Skela prison.

"Oh, great! Another prison," Johnny groaned. "I thought we already served our sentence. If I wanted to spend my life in prison, I could've stayed in Romania. They have plenty there."

"When I get out of here, I'll make sure I never spend another day in prison," I said.

Once again, we put our belongings into a little plastic bag and, once again, we were shoved into a large holding cell. Only this time, things would be different.

Although the holding cell was bigger than the last one, it was not big enough. Seventy Romanians were already occupying the room. Seventy.

The room got quiet as all eyes shifted to us, the news guys.

"Hey, Mark!" I heard someone shout.

I looked over and realized a boy I went to school with in Timişoara was the source of the call. "Emi, is that you?" I called back.

Emi squirmed his way through the crowd. He smiled as he firmly grasped my hand. "What's going on? I can't say I'm totally surprised to see you here!"

I, on the other hand, was very surprised to see Emi. As far as we all knew, Emi was a Communist party boy through and through. The word was he was one to watch out for if you had any anti-Communist sentiments. He was an informer. He went to the meetings and had the party membership I.D.

"I never thought I'd see you here," I said to him.

"Nah, man," he waved his hand down. "That was just a front. I said what they wanted to hear and pretended to care so I could stay under the radar. The guys I left with were in the party too," he said, pointing to his right. Whomever he pointed to, I had no idea. "Half the Communists don't believe that garbage. We did it for the benefits."

"You had me fooled."

"Good. That means I did a good job."

To say the room was overcrowded is an understatement. There were guys standing up, sitting on the floor and anywhere from two to three men napping on one bed sideways. But the mood was upbeat, a lot of laughter and cutting up.

"So, what's the deal?" I asked Emi. "I just spent 20 days in prison in some town near the border. Before getting here we were told we could go wherever we want. But instead we end up here."

"Basically, from what we've seen, if you're here, it means you're pretty much on your way to the other side," Emi explained.

"*Really?*"

"Uh-huh. They're always taking groups out of here and releasing them to the countries they want to go to. Be ready to tell them where you want to go. In a few days they're going to ask you."

"You can go anywhere?" I asked.

"You can go to New Zealand, Austria, Australia, Italy, Canada or America. Have you thought about where you want to go?"

"I think I've made up my mind already," I said.

"Where?"

"I've always wanted to go to Australia," I told him.

"Me too!" His eyes lit up. "I want to surf."

My reasoning for choosing Australia had nothing to do with surfing. For starters, the Australian dollar was strong, a factor I associated with a robust economy and jobs. Currency was something I'd kept up with for quite some time. It was especially an interest right before we fled, seeing as we planned on exchanging the wad of *lei* we let Florin take off with for the strongest currency possible. Secondly, I suspected the beautiful image of Melbourne I saw in the magazine as a child may have planted a seed, which had now sprouted. I envisioned the beautiful tropical scenery, the majestic city buildings, and a variety of vehicles traversing the landscape. The simplest, yet probably the strongest reason for my choosing Australia, was very practical: I wanted to get as far away from Romania as possible. I once stared at a map of the world for half an hour before actually measuring out which Western country was furthest from Romania. If someone was going to try and take me back, they would have to drag me through the ocean, across India, Pakistan, Afghanistan, Iran and Turkey, and finally, through the Black Sea.

Aside from Genu, the other guys also picked Australia. I don't know why Genu wanted to go to Italy. I'm not sure he did either. If he did, he certainly didn't tell me. I don't think it had anything to do with hard feelings toward us. He just liked the idea of Italy, I guessed. I later found out that Italy was not exactly open to receiving refugees in the way that Australia was. The way you got to Italy was different. You were taken to the border, dropped off, and basically told to run for it. Then you'd eventually be caught, you'd serve your sentence for entering illegally, and finally, be legally admitted into Italian society. Genu didn't know any of this at the time.

The Italy bus arrived before our Australia bus. We embraced and I wished Genu the best. "I wouldn't be here if it weren't for you," I told him.

Genu looked around, and through a smirk, said, "You have low standards."

I patted him on the shoulder and said, "You were the man with the plan. We had a hiccup or two along the way, but it wouldn't have happened without you."

"Thanks for talking to God for us that night. Sometimes, when I think about it, I still can't believe we weren't caught. You don't understand how unreal that was." He sighed. "I'm glad you took over when I froze. I'll always be glad I knocked on your door that day."

And just like that, Genu was gone.

My time at Padinska Skela was only bearable because of the hope in the atmosphere. I usually slept sideways next to Nick and Lucian. The food was just edible enough, and the atmosphere claustrophobic and foul. There was little bickering and practically no fighting, which is rare when you put so many Romanians together. Everyone was convinced a better life was just days away.

Although we didn't know it at the time, we later found out that we were waiting for the United Nations High Commissioner for Refugees to conduct our background checks and schedule our interviews with the respective consulates.

One night, the guard announced in Romanian, that my group of Australian-bound cohorts was scheduled to visit the Australian consulate tomorrow.

It was about time. I'd been in Padinska Skela prison for three weeks.

There was little preparing to do. It's not as if I had a suit I could put on and gel with which to sculpt my hair. I was still wearing the same clothes I left Romania in and my beard was coming out in patches. I wasn't the most impressive of sights. But I was confident the consulate representative would understand.

We were handed bus tickets, directions and food vouchers. The rest was up to us. If we were incapable of navigating through a strange city, we weren't the kind of refugees other countries wanted anyway. We were fortunate to have with us a young man who'd heard his parents speak Serbian as a child. For starters, he prevented us from boarding the wrong bus.

As the bus weaved around corners and sped by several tall buildings, I couldn't help but ruminate on what I saw. I was probably staring at the peaks of the soaring structures like a child who'd just seen the world's largest ice cream cone. It was all so new to me, seeing a city with so much activity and the stuff of cities. Little compact cars of all colors were speeding by in every direction, concession stands filled with magazines I'd never seen were scattered along the sidewalks, and meat seemed readily available at the passing piazzas. The number of motorcycles that *vroomed* by in Belgrade was surprising. There were people walking about, and others dined in the cafes.

The bus stopped and we quickly stepped off, scurrying to locate the consulate. We checked in and waited as a woman with big, blonde hair scrolled her index finger down a list of names. I sighed with relief as she read my name aloud.

"Tell me your background."

The interviewer spoke Romanian well for someone whose first language was English. He seemed relaxed, not a man who struck me as the worrisome type. If anything, he may have been slightly uninterested or distracted. I think I heard his stomach grumble.

"I am an electrician," I started. I went on about my training, where I went to school, and my experience as a high voltage electrician. I did not reveal to the monotone man how dispassionate I was about such work, or that I hated being an electrician. I also didn't tell him that I didn't plan to do such work in the future; the first opportunity I got to do something else I would hop on it like a cowboy in an American Western does on his horse.

"Tell me about your family. What do they do? What are they like?" he asked.

"My father works for the dynamite depository in Bozovici," I said. "My mother has just started working again, now that everyone has grown." I explained what my sisters were doing and about the jobs their husbands worked.

I talked for a good bit. The man periodically jotted notes on the sheet of paper in front of him. Even more infrequently, he glanced at a typed document to his left. "Uh-huh," he would occasionally say.

"Why Australia?"

Luckily, I'd been practicing. "I think Australia is a great country. It gives you opportunity and freedom, both things I am looking for. I am looking to work hard and be rewarded for it. And I'm tired of living in a country where people disappear, where those in charge do what they want and never have to answer to anybody. I don't think it's right. It's no way to live. I want to get as far away from Romania as possible. Australia is very far. I've measured it."

"Uh-huh." He put down his pen and turned his head up. "Well, Mark. Australia *is* a great country. And we have lots of opportunities for professionals such as you, people who want to work and earn what they work for. And as far as I know, we don't make a habit of grabbing people off the streets," he said, chuckling.

I laughed nervously.

He clasped his hands together and leaned back in his seat. He then let out a deep breath and stared at me for a few uncomfortable seconds.

"Mark, you're accepted," he finally said.

It was his decision to make. I assured him it was a good one as I shook his hand.

He made the same decision regarding all five of us.

- - -

We used the food vouchers to eat at one of the restaurants in the city. We drank a local beer to celebrate the occasion.

"Well boys," − I raised my glass − "we're off to Australia. Can you believe it?" We lifted our glasses and brought them together. Johnny pulled out a pack of cigarettes he won in a round of cards and passed it around. I lit mine right away. I stared out the window. We were actually going to the West. All the risk and delays were going to pay off. And the best part? We were done with prison. We only needed to wait on our passports to be made. That last phase of waiting would be done at a resort. Yes, a resort.

Banja Koviljača was a couple hundred miles outside of Belgrade. Tourists came to the town for the healing thermal mineral springs.

The resort was heaven on earth. I couldn't think of a better time to stay at one, considering I'd just spent the last six weeks in prison.

I shared a large, clean, and pleasant-smelling room with one other guy. We had vouchers for three meals a day, *any* three meals on the menu of the local restaurant. Breakfast seemed to be least emphasized.

Our choices usually came down to a few different pastries – meat or cheese – or jam-filled pastries and eggs any way you wanted, with tea or coffee. Lunch and dinner sometimes seemed similar to many dishes we ate in Romania. Foods like sausages and stuffed cabbage were Yugoslavian staples. There was always bread. I was introduced to new dishes like goulash and musaka.

During my stay at Banja Koviljača, I signed up for an English class that a professor from Timişoara taught in the common area of the hotel. He was a short, skinny man with large wire-rimmed glasses. He had escaped Romania many years ago with his teenage son.

"Now boys, the first thing you need to know about English is, unlike Romanian, it is rarely spelled how it sounds. There are some basic rules, but sometimes it will seem like there are no rules. Also, as is usually the case with any other language, there are approximately a million different dialects. This is especially the case with English. The English they speak in England is very similar to what they speak in America, Australia, New Zealand and South Africa, but there are also differences that go beyond accents. For instance, being a bomb in England is a good thing, whereas in America it is not something you want to say very loud. Also, if you ever drive a car and you notice a little light on the dash that says the BOOT IS OPEN, you'll know it's English because the only thing Americans know of boots is the ones they wear."

After three weeks of relaxing and watching TV at the resort, we were told our passports were completed. The flight to Australia was scheduled for the next week.

"You're going to have to move back to Belgrade, so you can be next to the airport," we were informed.

Once again, we were given bus tickets and directions. Our destination was a Belgrade hotel. We were to spend our last days in Yugoslavia there.

We were having lunch at a restaurant when a fedora-wearing stranger interrupted our conversation. He and his wife were behind us and overheard our conversation. The man was ethnically Romanian and ecstatic to hear the language of his childhood. He asked to hear our story of escape as he insisted they bring their chairs to our table, from where he listened intently. After a slight break in the narrative, he blurted out, "Mark, have you notified your family where you are? They must be terribly worried."

"No I haven't. I don't have any money," I told the man.

This peculiar, bearded old man fumbled through his pockets and pulled out a few dinars.

"Here, this should be enough to for you to buy a postcard and a stamp. Be a good son and notify your family as soon as possible."

I thanked the man, finished lunch, and walked to the one shop I knew had postcards. I grabbed one with a picture of Belgrade. I wrote:

> *Dad,*
> *I am in Belgrade. I am safe. Tomorrow*
> *I will be flying to Melbourne, Australia.*
> *-Mark*

"*Român ia*...stamp...*Român ia*," I told the shopkeeper.

He nodded and handed me what I asked for. "*Român ia*, huh?"

I nodded. "*Da.*"

The day before my departure I was in the common area, watching television and talking to people. The boy next to me was going to New York. He had always wanted to go to New York. He said Bob Dylan lived there. We had developed a friendship during the last few days. It occurred to me that by tomorrow I would be in a warm climate, whereas he would be in one much the opposite.

"I won't need this anymore," I told him, taking off my green parka. "It's summer in Australia."

The boy accepted the jacket and said he heard New York weather was similar to Romanian weather – cold. He wanted to give me something in return. He handed me a short-sleeved shirt. It wasn't anything special – just a light-blue, soft, buttoned shirt. It was hot and sunny in my new world. I would need lots of short-sleeved shirts. One was a good start.

PART II

-6-
THE WEST

Some things you just don't forget. Like the time I was in the garden with Dad, and all of sudden I heard the distinct roar of airplanes. Hovering over our heads was a fleet of Soviet planes on their way to Czechoslovakia. It was a magnificent sight. I wasn't sure if I should be impressed or scared.

Flight had always intrigued me, especially when it came to these large, heavy, man-made metal birds that carried hundreds of little people around this big planet at very high speeds. Airplanes changed the world. They not only changed how we warred, but how we traveled. Instead of months, airplanes made it possible to take only hours to go anywhere on the planet. Now I was on one. I was on my way to a place very far away.

I reminded myself of the planes I'd seen on that clear day in the field. They seemed to have little trouble staying up. But I quickly realized it was one thing to look at a plane and be convinced it was going to stay up when you're on the ground, and quite another to be inside one and have the same conviction. *A plane is so heavy…and so high up. What's to stop it from falling?*

The first leg of the flight to Australia concluded after just five hours of flying. We touched down in the Dubai airport. The doors of the JAT airplane opened and I was hit with a mighty wall of hot air. It wasn't sweltering, steamy air. It wasn't nasty, musty, humid air. It was just hot, as if God was blow-drying that particular parcel of the world. I definitely wasn't in Eastern Europe anymore.

The impression I got from walking around the Dubai airport was that this was what an airport was supposed to look like. All of a sudden I was an airport expert. First off, the airport was huge. Sure, I only had one other airport to compare it to, but I knew a big, fancy airport when I saw one. The benches and the terminals gleamed as if they'd been spit-shined. The glass reflected my image like a mirror. A choice of restaurants existed. And I could tell travelers regularly converged in this particular airport from all over the world.

We expected to see mostly people in turbans and traditional Middle Eastern wear. And we did see some of that. But there were also men and women in suits and others in casual jeans and t-shirts. I heard people speaking English, French, Italian and even German. And the ones that didn't sound like anything I'd ever heard, I assumed were Arabic. They were all in the Dubai airport, the owners of many different dialects, hurrying with their backpacks draped on their backs or their luggage rolling at their sides.

We grabbed a bench with a good view of the runway. We *ooo'ed* and *ahh'ed*, pointed and waved, and marveled at every fancy that tickled us, which was practically everything. Whoever spotted a plane bigger than the last one made sure the others didn't miss it. We stared at the people passing by. One man misconstrued our curiosity and yelled something at us before hurrying away.

We were in a new world. We were like kids who had finally escaped the clutches of an evil stepmother, indulging in all the candy we had been told we could never have. Of course we were going to point and stare.

"We're almost there," Nick said. "A few more hours and we'll be free."

"I thought we were already free," Lucian said.

"Well yeah, but you know what I mean. We'll be *totally* free."

"I considered myself free the moment I was out of Communist hands," Johnny cut in. He turned to me. "What do you think?"

"I guess I'm with you. I'm not sure. We're definitely freer now than we were before."

Australia was first discovered by Dutch explorers who regretted making the trip. It is said the reason the British were the ones to finally stake claim to it, almost 200 years later, was because they landed on the eastern coast and not the western. The west was mostly arid desert. The east had lush mountains with habitable landscape. The British initially used the large island as a penal colony. Thus Australia was born.

We hit Melbourne pavement 15 hours after leaving Dubai. It was 7:30 in the morning. The entirety of my passport was a page with my name and a picture. It was stamped by a customs agent who also affixed a red dot on the upper, left-hand side of my recently acquired shirt. We each got the dot. It was a sign for the man picking us up: *These guys with the dot, they're the dumb ones. Find them before they get lost.*

As we stood there dumbfounded, waiting, I noticed the only language I heard in this airport was English. There was no mishmash of anything else. I learned French in school and felt confident I could make my way in Italian if I had to. But aside from the *yes, no,* and *I love you* that I learned from cowboy movies and *Dallas,* I didn't recognize a single word. I didn't know how to ask anyone where I was supposed to go or what we were waiting for. The professor's few classes at the resort stuck to me like a father's advice to his young son.

Fortunately, we stayed put until a middle-aged man spotted our red dots and our confused looks, and came to our rescue. He yelled excitedly while striding toward us. He shook our hands as soon as he was in reach, revealing the widest grin I'd ever seen in Australia. We smiled and nodded back. *Yeah, yeah, we're happy, too.* He looked down at our feet and around. He clenched his fists, kept his arms parallel to each side, and picked up something invisible. Then he pointed toward us, and again picked up the invisible somethings.

"Oh! He's asking if we have any baggage," Nick said.

We shook our heads and shrugged our shoulders. "No. *Nu avem nimic!*"

"*Rien…niente…nimica.*" I wanted to drive the point home. We have nothing, friend.

"Come, come," he said, waving his hand.

We followed the man through the airport to his car, a blue sedan the size of which I'd never seen.

"This car is huge," I said aloud.

Johnny, who was now surveying the parking lot, said, "All the cars are so big. Look!"

We scanned the crammed airport parking lot. Hundreds of cars of all colors and shapes as far as we could see in every direction. The man, probably sensing we needed a minute, watched us in grinning fashion.

Although the car could've probably fit all five of us in the back seat, I decided I was going to sit in the front. I opened the right door and, to my surprise, found a steering wheel there. Jovial Man exploded with laughter when he saw my surprise. I guess it was his way of having fun with the whole thing. The other surprise was the column shifter and the lack of a stick shift on the floorboard. During the ride, I realized the car changed gears without the driver's help. It was an automatic. I'd heard of such contraptions and I remembered seeing one in a funny movie called *Uncle Marin the Billionaire.*

My initial impression as we rode through the suburbs of Melbourne was of order and peace. The lawns of the homes were meticulously manicured, the cars in the driveways with their polished wheels and glazed tires were immaculately clean, and the homes, though separate, lined up perfectly. And since it was Sunday it was rather quiet. I saw a few older folks watering plants, a walker or two here and there. Most of the stores were closed. The streets were sparsely populated. You could tell the city was taking it easy.

Jovial Man talked and pointed the entire ride, leaving us little space to discuss our assessment of our new world.

"What does he keep saying?" Johnny asked.

"Maybe he's giving us a tour," Nick suggested.

"But he knows we don't understand him."

"Clearly the talking is more for him than us. Let the man talk," I said, looking out my window.

Here I was, in a boat-sized car, driven by a man who couldn't stop smiling and talking, with my friends in the back bickering over whether the man should ease up on the chatter.

I made it.

We eventually arrived at the Resettlement of Refugees hostel in Maribyrnong, which was comprised of three gray, plain looking, two-story buildings. The grounds looked well-kept. The cement walls were unstained, the sidewalk free of debris, and the grass cropped and plentiful. The man stepped out of the car and signaled that we should follow him.

We were in luck. Not only was the young girl in the front office expecting us, but she happened to be Romanian. She was also a refugee; she worked there because she knew English.

The girl led us between the cement block halls of the buildings. "This place used to be a munitions factory of sorts," she informed us.

"You mean they made bombs here?" Lucian asked.

"Bombs, guns, grenades – sure."

Johnny made a joke about maybe finding a left-over machine gun in an overlooked part of the building.

"Are we allowed to stay here?" I asked.

"*Da*. That's what this place is for. You are to stay here until you can make it on your own. And don't worry. You're not only getting housing, but also food and some pocket money. Breakfast is from 6 - 9 a.m., lunch from 11 a.m. – 1 p.m. and dinner from 5 – 7 p.m. Also, take note. Twice a week there are English classes you can take. It would be in your best interests to show up and do the work. This isn't Romania. Nobody is going to make you go, or wake you up. You're free to come and go, but if you end up a bum, then it's on you."

"What's that smell?" I asked. It was so potent…and foreign.

"You mean the food?" she asked.

"That's food?" Nick asked.

"Although we have a cafeteria, a lot of the refugees here like to prepare their own food. They buy small portable grills and cookware to make food in their rooms. Yes, Oriental food has a distinctive, strong smell. I suppose I've gotten used to it."

"Are they all from China?" Lucian asked, peeking into the rooms with the open doors.

"No. The Asians here all pretty much come from Vietnam, Cambodia and Laos. The Vietnamese started coming in by the boatloads a few years ago, after the Communists took over their country. I'm sure you guys can relate."

The last part of the tour was the convenience store. It was stacked with all sorts of goodies. I bought a pack of cigarettes and a Coke. I had a Pepsi-Cola before, but never a Coca-Cola. I was about to see what all the rage was about.

There was one entrance for every two rooms, which were separated by the bathroom. Everyone got their own small room, complete with a bed, nightstand, dresser, and a window to the outside world, which also doubled as a release for the overpowering aroma in the air. I was assigned to share my bathroom with the Serbian-Romanian young man I met in Belgrade. Toothbrushes, toothpaste and soap were neatly lined up on the bathroom mirror shelf. Folded white towels were stacked in a small basket in the corner.

I took a deep breath and looked out the window, taking in the view from the second story. It wasn't much, just the side of another building. But it was the view beyond I was really thinking of.

Nick, Lucian and Johnny came in to see if my apartment was as cool as theirs. It was exactly as cool, they reassured me.

"I can't believe we're here," Nick said, looking out the window. "I can't wait to call my ex and talk to my son."

"I hope my parents got my postcard. I hope they don't think I'm dead," I added.

"I don't think I'm going to let anyone know where I am," Johnny said.

We were interrupted by sudden knocking. Everyone got quiet and turned their attention to the door. *Knock, knock.*

"...yes?"

The door slowly opened as a man with thinning gray hair slipped his average build in the partial opening. *"Bună dimineaţa băieţi!"*

Without thinking, I answered back in Romanian. "Good morning."

"May I come in?" he asked.

I turned and saw Nick and Lucian suspiciously staring at the man. Lucian was leaning on the dresser. Johnny went to use the bathroom just seconds before, and upon the man's arrival, decided to stay there. There's no way, I thought. No way they could've followed and located us so quickly. I also reasoned that if they were going to send someone for us, it wouldn't be a frail, old man.

"Sure…" I said, a little uneasy. "You may come in." We could hear the tenants down the hall laughing. No one in our room made a sound.

"My name is Toma Toma," the man said, breaking the silence. He extended out his right hand. I shook it.

"What are you doing here, Toma Toma?" Nick asked.

"I'm here to invite you to a *gathering,*" he said, smiling.

"*Gathering?*" It had been a long time since I heard that word.

"Yes. We're a small group of Romanians here in Melbourne—"

"Romanians?" I asked.

"Yes," he answered.

"Here? In Australia?" I asked again.

"Yes." Toma Toma's eyes shifted around the room. "Romanians here in Australia." He smiled. "I come here to the hostel often, to welcome new Romanians. The girl at the desk told me where to find you. We are a small group of people who get together and fellowship every Sunday. Would you all like to— "

Just then Johnny came out of the bathroom door. "Hello."

"I'm Toma Toma," the man said. "I was just telling your friend…."

"I heard," Johnny said.

"I don't know, Mr. Toma," Nick said. "We just got off the plane. We've been traveling for 20 hours. We're tired and hungry."

"Hungry?" The man's gentle eyes widened. "That's perfect. At the end of our service we will be having food. Good Romanian food," Toma said, grinning again.

"Did you say food?" I asked.

"I could eat," Lucian said, looking at Nick.

"What else happens at these *gatherings*?" I asked.

"Oh, you know. We sing a song or two, pray a prayer or two, listen to a sermon, and have a little fellowship. That's what we do."

"Oh. You're talking about church," I said.

"Yes. Church. And we would be honored if you joined us. We can easily fit everyone in my car."

"I have no doubt. We've seen the cars here," Nick said.

"Tell me more about this food," I said.

"Soup, sausage, stuffed cabbage, mashed potatoes – desserts of all kinds." Toma rattled off a list of goodies. Every one of them sounded better than the last. I hadn't had Romanian stuffed cabbage since I went home last Easter.

"Johnny, are you coming?" I asked.

"I don't know, guys." He was doing his squinting-one-eye-bobbing-his-head-back-and-forth routine. "I'm not much of a church man. I think I'll stay here and get some sleep."

In the car, Toma Toma informed us that the pastor of the church we were about to visit was new to Australia. Five months new, to be exact. He was fresh from Banat. But we had more pressing matters to be addressed.

"Hey, how come you have two first names…and they're both the same?" This apparently had been bothering Lucian ever since we met the man. "Did you change your name to hide from Communists? Or is it a nickname?"

"No, boys. Both names were the ones I was given. My parents named me Toma and my family name is Toma. I'm not sure if my first name was shortened or if I was being called by my last name. But now everyone calls me Toma Toma."

"You said the pastor is from Banat. What's his name?" I asked, satisfied with the man's explanation.

"Are you from Banat?" Toma asked.

"You could say that. I went to school and worked in various parts of Banat. My sister lives there now, in Timişoara."

Toma adjusted his sunglasses as he made a wide right. "The pastor's name is Claudiu Gheorghe. He's a great guy."

"*Claudiu Gheorghe!*" I exclaimed.

"Uh-huh."

"I think I know him! I met him at my sister's wedding."

"Small world," the man replied.

- - -

The First Romanian Baptist Church of Australia off Stanley Street reminded me of the ages it had been since I'd stepped foot inside a church.

There was a mandolin orchestra and a choir on opposite sides of the platform. The orchestra had more girls than the choir. One mandolin-playing girl in particular caught my eye. I don't know if it was because she was sitting in the front row or because I caught her looking at me. I thought she tried to play it off and make it look like she was scanning the entire chapel. I couldn't help but look at the pretty dark-haired girl – perhaps too long.

When I saw the pastor, Claudiu Gheorghe, behind the pulpit, I was reassured. I had definitely met him at my sister Petra's wedding. I traveled halfway around the world and in no more than two hours after landing I was surrounded by Romanians. What were the chances?

The pastor was talking about "moving around." A lot of the moving around people do in life is, at its core, a search for significance, for truth, he bellowed. "If I could just get there, if I could just get that," he explained, "then I would be satisfied." He wiped his brow with a white handkerchief. It was summer in Australia.

"Brothers and sisters, I'm here to tell you that significance can only come from one place, and that is Jesus Christ!" Gheorghe thundered.

I was tired. I was comfortable and relaxed in my seat. It's like I'd been here before. This church was a place where I could relax and be at ease.

"Australia, Romania, America – the Lord Jesus is everywhere! And, therefore, significance is everywhere. He isn't limited by governments, or anything else!" Gheorghe thundered. Then he smiled. "I know, I know. Some of you are thinking, 'Well, Pastor, Jesus Christ may be everywhere, but I think in Romania, the Communists are hiding Him.'" I heard chuckling.

I looked over to my friends. Lucian was lazily gazing in the direction of the orchestra, and Nick was flipping through the hymnal, maybe hoping there was a connection between the speed at which he flipped the pages and the passing of time.

My friends, however, came alive in the cafeteria. They joked with the girls serving the food, shook hands with everyone, and voraciously devoured the stuffed cabbage. In the meantime, I went back for seconds. I wanted to know the name of the girl I'd seen in the front row. She didn't smile when I asked her name. She looked at me very seriously, as if to inform me that she was immune to my charm. She looked down toward my ankles and sharply said, "Christine." Without pausing, she asked if I'd like more green beans.

"That's enough," I told her.

Among the people who welcomed us was the pastor. Smiling, he walked to our table, introduced himself, shook our hands, and asked us our names. When he heard my last name his eyes widened.

"Hobafcovich?" he asked.

"Yes." My mouth was full.

"You wouldn't happen to be from Bozovici, would you?"

"I am," I replied, taking a sip of orange soda.

"Your sister, Petra, is married to a very good friend of mine. We met at her wedding, you and I. Remember? You have definitely grown a foot or two since."

"I'm glad to have grown. Actually, I was telling the man who drove us here the same thing, the part about knowing you, that is. What are the chances?"

On our way out of the church a man named Simon stopped to talk to us. He was pleased to hear I was from Bozovici. He was from Moldova Noua. We were both from the same county of Caraş-Severin. He was a few years older than me. I noticed he was missing three fingers on his left hand. I think he noticed my noticing.

"I'm a carpenter," he said, looking at his hand.

"Does it hurt?" I asked.

"No. It just feels like the old fingers are still there."

After a few more minutes of talking, he asked me where I was staying. The other guys were in the car, waiting.

"We're at the hostel in Maribyrnong," I told him.

"Oh, that's too far," he said.

Too far for what? I thought.

"We need to move you," he said.

"Move me? You can do that?"

"There's another refugee hostel closer; in Springvale. Tomorrow I can pick you up and transfer you. Is that okay?" He didn't give me a chance to answer. "From Springvale I may be able to find you a job, maybe even help you get back and forth for a little while."

Despite Pastor Gheroghe's sermon, it appeared moving around may have done me some good after all. The ink from the stamp on my passport was still drying and there was already talk of a job.

"What can you do?" Simon asked.

I rattled off a list of what I had done, what I could do and what I wouldn't mind doing.

"Can you weld?" he asked.

"Yes, I can." I forgot to mention that.

"Good. I know someone at GMH. He's a Swiss with a soft heart for Eastern Europeans. He may be able to help you get a job," he said.

"Why does he like Eastern Europeans?" I asked.

"He visited Romania years ago. I think he may feel sorry for us a little bit. 'Rich country, poor management,' is his assessment. He thinks we Romanians do good work," Simon explained.

GMH, or GM Holden Ltd., is responsible for General Motor's market in Australia. Holden was the make of the car the man who picked us up from the airport was driving. Holden was the car I saw most on the highways and streets of Australia.

"Have your stuff ready tomorrow morning," Simon hollered as I lowered into Toma's car. "I'll be there at eight."

That was easy. My stuff was all ready to go. I was wearing it.

The others had been waiting on me. "Are you going somewhere, Mark?"

"It appears so," I said, though I thought it a bit strange that the two-fingered fellow was so eager to help me.

When we got back to the hostel, Johnny was fully refreshed. While we were at church he napped, so he was ready to hit the town. He suggested we go somewhere and have a beer, in full Aussie fashion.

"It sure is hot enough for a beer," Nick said.

We asked the girl at the desk where we could go for a beer. We were in a celebrating mood, we told her.

"Nowhere today," she said.

"What do you mean?" Nick asked.

"You can't buy alcohol on Sundays."

"What?!"

"That's the law," she said in an irritated fashion. "I already told your friend." She looked at Johnny.

"I thought you meant here. As in, we can't buy beer here, not *everywhere*," Johnny said.

After walking the surrounding streets in hope of proving the girl wrong, we conceded defeat and bought candy and Cokes from the hostel store instead. We found an unoccupied bench outside and occupied it.

"This will have to do," I said, looking out.

"We'll get beer tomorrow," Johnny said.

"I'm leaving tomorrow," I said.

"Already? We just got here." Lucian said.

"Is that guy taking you somewhere else?" Nick asked.

"Yeah, another hostel. He says he can get me a job, but I need to move closer."

"Why is he doing all this?" Lucian asked.

"I don't know," I said. "I really don't know."

"Well, tell him I like to work, too," Nick said, patting me on the back.

"I'll pass it on."

Moving me from one refugee hostel to another was as easy as suggesting it to the front offices of both hostels. There were no objections. I signed one paper, Simon another, and the girl in the office stamped both. "Good luck," she said as we trotted out.

The way things worked in Australia would take some getting used to. I was allowed to come and go as I pleased. There appeared to be little to no top-down oversight. From the office to the kitchen, even the various training courses, the hostels were run by refugees and common folk, most of whom had been refugees themselves. If I was going to learn English, I'd better show up and take notes. Nobody was going to hold my hand. There was no penalty for not showing up because nobody kept count. No one told you what to use your allowance for. No one told you what you could and could not read. No one asked you to check in and out as you left the hostel. And no one said you couldn't cook whatever you wanted to in your own room.

On our way to Springvale, I asked Simon what he thought the chances would be of my having to live in a constant fog of sweet and sour smells.

"Pretty good. Those hostels are packed with Southeastern Asians. They're all pretty much fleeing the same system we did. You should try the food. It's not that bad. I ate it when I stayed there."

The Springvale hostel looked like a replica of Maribyrnong, from the cement blocks to the tidiness of the lawn.

"Sunday morning. I'll see you then. In the meantime, relax. Enjoy the week. Eat some pho. Read your Bible," Simon yelled before speeding off in his big white station wagon.

Relaxing would include playing soccer with my fellow refugees and sharing in their cuisine. I couldn't understand a word they were saying. Not that it mattered. When I scored a goal, it was clear from the shouts and laughing we were speaking the same language. In the cafeteria they always wanted to put more on my plate than I wanted. I didn't need words to understand their generosity.

I was eventually driven to my only source of understandable language, my *Biblia*. Before leaving, the First Romanian Baptist Church of Australia gave my friends and me each a Romanian Bible. Now I was in a place where that Bible was the only thing I could connect with. I'd read the Bible before. There was always one around when I was young. But it had been years.

Pastor Gheorghe inspired me. So did Toma Toma. Simon's strange generosity was especially intriguing. They seemed like genuinely nice people. But I was a little suspicious of their friendliness. Maybe their kindness had something to do with their professed faith, I thought.

I opened my new Bible and begin skimming through the books of Matthew, Mark, Luke and John between soccer games and smoke breaks.

The next week, Simon, staying true to his word, picked me up for church. Aside from the mandolin-playing girl, I was looking forward to seeing my traveling companions and telling them about my new appreciation for Oriental cuisine. I was sad to see that none of them were there.

After church, I was invited over for lunch by a man in a gray suit. His name was Peter Velja. Peter and Anna, his wife, had 15-year-old twins Christine and David, the same Christine who had stared at my ankles and given me a second helping of green beans.

My first impression of the Velja home was that it was a palace. It was roomy – no doubt the vast family area helped – spotless, and furnished with what seemed the finest furniture I'd ever seen. What stood out most was the billiard table in one of the rooms. A pool table in a private home? Who knew?

Peter's wife and daughter had already set the table by the time we arrived. David appeared from his room. The family, with me in the middle, gathered around the table. Peter prayed over the food and we began eating.

David and Christine spoke to their parents only in Romanian, and the parents vice versa. Christine and David's Romanian accent reminded me of the Australian consul I interviewed with in Belgrade. I was surprised to hear so much Romanian spoken in the home, especially once I learned that the twins were born in Australia.

Peter's daughter was, indeed, very pretty. I was sure my sentiment was unrequited. It seemed she went out of her way to avoid making eye contact. She kept her eyes on her plate and when she did say something, it was always to someone on the opposite side of the table. I was probably just a charity case her dad brought home, a scrawny, smelly puppy who needed a meal and an etiquette lesson. When she and David were talking, I did pick up the word "cigarette." Although I thought I concealed my habit well, I now had reason to reconsider. I guess the secret was out. I don't think Peter's daughter was impressed.

"Mark, how's the food?" Anna asked.

"Fantastic. You have no idea how much of a welcome change this food is for me."

"If you don't mind, tell us a little about you – your family, your background. You seem like a very nice, intelligent young man. I want to know how you got be that way," the man at the head of the table said.

I told them a little about Bozovici, my parents, growing up in the Bozovici church and about where I went to school.

"So once you went to Reșița you stopped going to church?" Peter asked.

David said something to Christine. Christine hit David in the shoulder. Peter looked over at them and they stopped.

"There was just no time," I said.

"Hmm." Peter nodded.

"I hear Simon arranged an interview at GMH tomorrow. That's really nice of him. How do you think you're going to do?" Anna asked.

"I'll do well. I'm excited about working, about making money." I grabbed one of the *mititei* on my plate, dipped it in mustard, and bit into it.

"How are you on clothes?" Peter asked.

"What do you mean? I keep my clothes clean and, so far, they haven't torn," I answered.

"What I meant is: do you have any other clothes?"

Peter, I learned, was a tailor by trade. He worked at a high-end department store. He was called Dr. Velja by his clients because he was so good at what he did. High-powered executives who needed to look their best worked only with Peter. He had an uncanny eye for fitting and assorting people into just the right outfit. Clients made an appointment for a suit. Peter would not only sell them a suit, he'd sell them an arsenal of shirts, ties and socks to go with the suit. Peter must have noticed I was wearing the same clothes I wore last Sunday.

"We're going to need to do something about that," he said. "I know someone exactly your size."

"Okay." I wasn't sure what exactly that meant. I was distracted. "I've never seen a billiard table in anyone's house."

"Do you play?" David asked.

"Not as much as I like."

"We can play after lunch," Peter said.

After lunch, David kicked my butt. Then it was Peter's turn. He took it easy on me. I almost won.

Peter asked if I'd like a nice, cold drink to console me. I acquiesced. He suggested we drink it in the other room.

He had taken off his tie and jacket.

"What are you going to do with all this?" he asked, looking out. He sipped his glass.

I looked at the beautiful home across the street. "All of what?"

"This freedom. That's why you came here, right?" Another sip.

"Yes."

"Is it everything you hoped it would be?" He looked over at me. There was something very genuine and warm about the man. Something about him reminded me of my own father.

"I guess it's too early to tell. I think I will have a job by tomorrow, and when that goes well, I plan on getting a place, maybe a car after that. I think that's good for now." I downed the last of my orange drink. "Right?"

"Sure it is. It's good to get settled, make money, build a career. Nothing wrong with any of it. Lord knows He has blessed me with all of it and more. But what I'm trying to get to," he sighed, "is to help make sure you don't end up like so many other young Romanians. I've seen so many bright, young men come here and become enslaved all over again."

"Enslaved? Here?"

"Yes. They get tied down to alcohol, drugs, the wrong women, the materialism that is so common in the West. Don't be fooled, Mark. We have our own problems here."

"Hmm."

"Before you know it, you'll be in debt up to your eyeballs; you'll be drinking every night to forget it; and you'll have a nagging wife you married for the wrong reasons. Now you've run out of hope because there's nowhere left to run. This was supposed to be the Promised Land. But all you've done is traded one slave master for another. I see it happen all the time," Peter said.

"This place has everything, compared to Romania," I said. "In the little bit of time I've been here, I noticed a lot more happy and generous people. But maybe you're right. It's not necessarily the stuff that brings happiness...although you do have a lot of stuff. One thing I have noticed is the peace in your home."

"Where do you think that peace comes from?"

"I think it's a result of the absence of fear. In Romania people live in fear. Not so much here," I said.

"Mark, over time you will find plenty of people – even here – without peace in their lives and homes, many destroyed lives…."

"Maybe, but…."

"The peace you noticed in our home has nothing to do with our stuff," Peter said. "There are people with twice the stuff and nowhere near the peace. I meet them every day. Sometimes I feel like their therapist, not their personal stylist."

"Then what does it have to do with, this peace?" I asked.

"It comes from Jesus Christ. I'll be straight with you, Mark. I see a lot of myself in you. I grew up in the same kind of home as you. Then I changed the first chance I got. Just like you. But I never stopped searching. You and I, we're like that. We can't help but search, always hoping to find another missing link. But it's not really searching as the world would like to tell you. It's being pursued. We're simply responding. I think there is a reason God allowed you out of Romania. You have to figure out why."

Gheorghe said it was significance that came from Jesus. Now Peter was saying peace came from Jesus, too. It seemed like many good things involved Jesus. And it seemed to me that Jesus was awfully busy.

- - -

My interview at GMH was a test to see if my claim that I could weld was true. Simon picked me up, drove me to the plant and introduced me to The Big Swiss. Since I couldn't communicate in English, Simon interpreted for us.

I put on the protective mask, grabbed the "gun" with my left hand and waited to get the electrode in my other.

"There you go. Let's see what you got," Simon said, looking down at the pieces of metal The Big Swiss had laid down in front of me.

"Okay." I shrugged my shoulders. "I'm waiting on you." I looked over at The Big Swiss. He just stood there, arms crossed. I looked at Simon. He was looking at me. "Well? Where's the electrode?"

"There isn't one. Not like that anyway. This is MIG welding. I thought you said you knew how to weld."

"Not with this. I've never seen this in my life!" I was holding the foreign object in my hand as if I had just unearthed an ancient fossil.

The Big Swiss said something to Simon. My heart rate began rising. I couldn't afford to botch this opportunity. I needed this job. Who knew when the next opportunity would arrive? I did not want to stay at the hostel one more day than necessary.

Then, as if God himself gave me a nudge, I reminded myself that whether MIG or stick welding, the concept of welding was still the same. The means were a little different, but the result needed to be the same. I snapped my mask on, bent over and pulled the trigger. What did I have to lose?

A wire came out as I pulled the trigger. I cautiously neared the sheets of metal. Here goes nothing, I thought. I found myself welding by faith.

My faith paid off. Once I'd worked all the way down the adjoining metal sheets, The Big Swiss came over and inspected the work. He hunched down and worked his head up the point of convergence. He then slowly stood up straight and looked at me. His face muscles were forcibly relaxed, as if he was a gambler trying to hide a tell. But he broke and grinned.

Simon smiled. "He says it's good. Seamless. Very good. Are you sure you never MIG welded?"

I wiped my brow and took a deep breath. "You think I wanted to go through that? Did I get the job?"

I looked over at The Big Swiss as Simon was translating. He smiled at me. Then he shook my hand.

"You have to fill out some paperwork."

On our way back to the hostel, Simon bought me lunch.

It suddenly hit me. "Simon!" I exclaimed.

I startled him.

"I don't have a car. How am I supposed to get to work?" The distance was too far to consider walking.

"I'll take you until we figure something out," he said nonchalantly.

"Really? You'll do that?"

"Yeah, why not?" he answered.

On the eight day after my arrival in Australia I began working.

-7-

A NEW LIFE

If my memory serves me well, Gheorghe had four children around the table. Maybe five. One of them hit me in the stomach and ran away. Whatever the count, most of them were young and rambunctious. They were all over the place. I may have counted the same one twice.

Surprisingly, when it came time to eat you would think the place had suddenly become a monastery. Although a seemingly patient woman, Gheorghe's wife *demanded* respect. She had the ability to shut her children up with a death-stare capable of raising shivers down the backs of the hardest men.

I spent my third Sunday afternoon in Australia in Pastor Claudiu Gheorghe's home. By this time, I suspected the church's leaders had designated someone to take and feed me every Sunday. I had no qualms about home-cooked meals. Whatever their motivation, the food tasted all the same: painstakingly and mouth-wateringly delicious. Despite living alone for so many years, I never arrived at a point where I could confidently claim to know how to cook. At least not anything anyone else would want to eat. I was more of a survival cook. I could fry up an egg, put a sandwich together, maybe cut up a few vegetables, boil them, and call it soup. But even that was a stretch.

Since he was the first Romanian pastor actually shipped in from the old country to Melbourne, I asked him how in the world he managed to convince the Communists to not only allow *him* out, but his entire family with him. He said he had been sponsored by the church in Australia. In short, the Romanian government decided it was worth letting him out for the money they got in return. This wasn't anything new, I was informed. It was a form of ransoming. During the late sixties, the Norwegian Mission to the Jews and the Hebrew Christian Alliance ransomed a man named Richard Wurmbrand out of Romania for $10,000. The going rate for political prisoners was $1,900. It appeared even the Communists couldn't help but take advantage of capitalism.

Wurmbrand eventually moved to America, where he one day gained an audience before the United States Senate's Internal Security Subcommittee. He used the opportunity to quail any optimism about the treatment of dissident religious and political leaders behind the Iron Curtain. He took his shirt off his gouged and scarred back for everyone in the chamber to see.

But Gheorghe didn't want to spend the afternoon talking about Wurmbrand.

"Mark, I heard you started working at GMH," he said.

"I did."

"How's is it going so far?"

"It's good. I'm on a welding team with two other guys. Both of them, Fred and John, are really nice. John is the team leader. He's an older guy, very good at what he does. He's a welding machine. Fred is the other guy. He has really long hair. They go out and drink beer almost every day after work."

Gheorghe smiled. "Do you ever go with them?"

"No. They haven't invited me. They're probably waiting until I can speak English."

"I must give it to them. Slurred speech sounds a lot better in English than in Romanian," Gheorghe said, chuckling.

"I never was much of a beer drinker anyway," I said.

"Australians love their beer," said Gheorghe.

"I noticed."

"These bars, pubs they call them, are full everyday after everyone gets off work."

"Claudiu…?" His wife gave him a look.

"Oh, right." He wiped his lip. "One thing we can always do is pray for them, hoping one day they'll be on the straight and narrow."

Gheorghe's face suddenly lit up. "Mark, Mark! Have you called any of your family in Romania since you've been here?"

"Well…no. My parents don't have a phone," I said.

"What about your sister, Petra? I know she does. Let's call her right now."

In giddy fashion, Gheorghe came out of the other room carrying a gray rotary phone. Along with a small notebook of phone numbers, he set the phone on the only clean corner of the table. "I hope it's not too late to call," he said with his head down and eyes feverishly scrolling through the names.

I didn't think of calling my sister because I didn't want to get her in trouble, I excused to Gheorghe. The truth was I simply didn't see the big deal in calling.

Gheorghe dismissed the notion that we might get Petra in trouble. "They" only track families of those with valuable information, or the ability to really hurt the State. Romania doesn't have the manpower to harass every family member of everyone who defects, he explained.

Smiling from ear to ear, he made the rounds on the phone, number by number. He looked up at me as he put the receiver to his left ear. "It's ringing," he said, smiling. I took another bite of cake.

"Hello! This is Claudiu Gheorghe from Australia…I hope I'm not calling too late…I am good…how are you? Petra, listen. I have someone here who'd like to talk to you…." He handed me the phone.

"Hello Poosha," I said. Poosha was her nickname.

There was no sound on the other end. "Poosha, are you there?" I heard a faint whimpering.

"Are you in Australia? I mean…of course you are, but…but… what are you doing in Australia?" She backed away from the receiver. "It's Mark. I think he's in Australia," I heard her say.

"I'm here. I'm safe and sound. Calm down." It sounded like she was hyperventilating.

"We thought you were dead! Dad asked your neighbors, your boss – he asked *everyone*, Mark! Nobody knew what happened to you! We thought you were dead!"

"I'm not dead. I'm alive. I promise. I sent a postcard before leaving Belgrade. I'm guessing Dad never got it…?"

"Belgrade? Postcard? No. No one got a postcard. Why were you in Belgrade?" she asked.

I gave her a condensed version of our escape. I didn't tell her names, or the route we took.

"Listen, Poosha," I said. "Tell Mom and Dad I am well. Tell them not to worry. I have to go," I said.

"Of course. Of course, I will. And don't forget to write."

"Bye."

"That should put your family at ease. God only knows the turmoil they've been going through," Gheorghe said.

I felt like a selfish jerk. I shouldn't have waited so long to call them.

- - -

I was asked by a few other guys at church if I wanted to live with them. They were more or less my age. I would get out of the hostel and they would pay less rent. Everyone would be a winner.

Although my new roommates had been in Australia a little longer than me, they were still considered WOGS. WOGS was an acronym used to refer to Eastern European immigrants. The original is said to have stood for Westernized Oriental Gentlemen. Although I didn't understand how the "Oriental" part applied to us, I liked the gentlemen part. By the time it had been applied to us, however, the term had been through centuries of cultural amendments. My roommates noted my ignorant satisfaction and immediately informed me that being called a WOG was *not* a good thing. He then used a very ineloquent parallel to racist terms Romanians apply to certain ethnic minorities to illustrate his point.

"Oh, yeah! Is there anything we can call them back?" I asked, offended to be on the receiving end of ethnic prejudice.

"You can call them 'skips,'" my roommate, Gaius, answered.

"What does that mean?" I asked.

"I don't know, but I've heard that's what they call themselves. I think it has something to do with kangaroos, you know, because they skip." Gaius hopped two fingers on the banister to illustrate a kangaroo skipping along.

"What's the point in calling them something they like?" I asked. "Anyway, I don't think I care. The whole thing seems dumb anyway."

The decision to move out of the hostel was a no-brainer. I'd received my first payment for work and I wasn't wasting any time moving up in the world. It turned out that I was a pretty good welder. The Big Swiss was so impressed with me that, later on, he arranged a welding challenge between me and my two team members. He did this to illustrate that he believed me up to par with the other men. In the first round, I beat out both John and Fred. I won. This may have been more hurtful to John than Fred. Fred was not really into it. But John, the old pro, made sure I didn't win the next round.

Another benefit to my new place was its location. It was within walking distance from the bus station. The bus station would allow me to get to work. This was also good news for Simon. I appreciated him immensely, but I didn't want to rely on him all the time. The man had done enough. It was time I carried my own weight.

I would miss an occasional Sunday here and there, but since the morning Toma Toma picked me up from the hostel in Maribyrnong, I showed up at the little Romanian church just as much as I didn't.

I had a good reason for the times I didn't show up. The more I went to church, and talked to church people, and ate with church people, and laughed with church people, the more apparent it became that a problem was brewing. Church was beginning to make me uncomfortable. It made me feel bad about myself. I didn't like that. I believed feeling bad about myself was a result of some of the things Gheorghe was preaching. Other reasons had to do with the contrast in my lifestyle and those of the people I met at church. They thought and talked a little different. They behaved a little different. Not all of them, but most of them. They believed sex outside of marriage was wrong, getting drunk was wrong, being selfish was wrong, and even smoking was wrong. They abstained from those things. They also didn't swear or tell dirty jokes. What am I doing here? I sometimes asked myself. I shouldn't be affected the way I am. I'd known good people like these all of my first 14 years on Earth and they never bothered me before. So why was this time different?

I considered putting a halt to my church attendance. Maybe I would stop feeling bad. I didn't risk my life crossing the world just to be told, once again, how wrong I was. I could've stayed in Romania for that prognosis.

As appealing and tempting staying away from church was, I had a semi-conscious knowing, an urging of sorts, that doing so would be the worst thing I could do. It was as if some force was pulling me in its direction and I was powerless to resist. As bad as "that direction" was making me feel, deep down I knew it was a *good* bad feeling.

It wasn't as if anyone was directly accusing me. No one was badgering me or hitting me on the head with their Bibles. No one sneered at me because my clothes smelled of cigarette smoke. No one asked me how many beers I had this past week. Nobody was interested in how many questionable relationships I had in the past. What they did was feed me, talk to me and drive me when I needed to go somewhere. They accused me with their actions. But that was enough.

Moreover, I still hadn't found an ulterior motive for these people's ongoing generosity. I still questioned the niceness of the people in Australia. It was so new, so strange. I couldn't help but believe they wanted more than my well-being. But what?

Unless…

What if the crummy feelings I was experiencing *were* the ulterior motive? Could it be that the church people conspired to make me feel bad by being super generous? Could it be they somehow subconsciously manipulated me into reading the Bible with the force of generosity and home cooked meals, all so they could swell up their congregation numbers and influence in the Romanian community of Melbourne?

I took my gnawing doubts to the closest person by, my roommate Gaius. Maybe he could help.

"That's ridiculous! There's no way they're that clever and disciplined," he scoffed. "I don't know what you're really talking about, Mark. I've gone to that church several times, and I don't feel bad about anything. I must be immune to their 'clever tactics.' I don't know what *your* problem is. Maybe you're adjusting to life here a little differently." He took a swig from his beer.

"Maybe Peter was right. Maybe God *was* real and actually pursuing me," I said.

Gaius looked at me, puzzled. "Sure, He's real. He's out there, somewhere. He's in the stars and the moon. He's in that tree," he pointed. "Maybe He's in this beer. Man, I don't know. He's somewhere...or something. But as far as Him coming after you, that I don't know. It sounds weird, God doing something like that."

It occurred to me that for my entire life I just assumed God. The idea of God was something so ingrained throughout my upbringing that I never really questioned my exact ideas of God. I looked at God as a generic forest without any individual trees. For so long, God was an ambiguous Being, high in Heaven, Who always spoke and did things in the life of people I heard about but never knew. He was a safety net should all the heaven and hell talk be real.

But I was starting to attach a real Being to God. A Being with likes and dislikes, with feelings of anger, of joy, with actions of wrath and actions of love. The trees were coming into focus. The irony was, up to this point, I had thought of everything else – from natural rights to the predispositions responsible for birthing rebels and pioneers and followers. And now everything was coming together, and ultimately, pointing to God.

Unlike Gaius, Peter thought God was more than a mystery component in beer and asteroids. "From the freedom I enjoy here in Australia to the satisfaction I find in my job, God gets the credit," he said. "And if you want to know something about God's personality, look at Jesus. He was God in human flesh."

The thing about Peter, which was uncommon for older folks I'd met, was that he spoke on my level. I didn't feel like he was talking down to me. Our conversations felt real, as if between two friends who went to school together.

One day when I was seven or eight, back in Bozovici, I had been helping my sister, Mary, watch our few sheep. At some point, I heard the cry of a sheep coming from the direction of the river. I told Mary I was going to investigate. She told me to stay away from the river and to "get back here!" We just had a lot of rain and the river was especially dangerous. I was her responsibility.

"Don't worry," I said. "I'll be careful."

The cry came from a black lamb struggling to hang on to a rock settled on the river bank. Black lambs were rare. We didn't know anyone else who had one. It was certainly not ours.

The little guy was drenched and terrified. He wouldn't stop crying. *Beh-heh-heh!* I cautiously stepped forward through the mud, my feet sinking a little with each step. *Beh-heh-heh!* I went near enough to secure one hand on each side of his belly. Gathering all my strength I tugged. I felt him trying to hold onto the rock. The little lamb had no idea I was trying to save his life. Fortunately for him, there was nothing to give him traction. I easily lifted him up and brought him to my chest and stepped back to safety.

We never did find out to whom he belonged. We asked our neighbors and no one had a black lamb. So we adopted him into our flock.

A couple years later, that same river would present an opportunity for another rescue.

There's a part where the two rivers, the Nera and the Minis, come together. Again, we had just had torrential rains. The rivers had flooded. My friends and I occasionally played in the river. Trying to outdo everyone else, I thought it would be a good idea to climb the branch of a tree right above the spot where the two rivers converge, where the water was deepest. What I failed to consider was the part the whirlpool in that spot would play.

The moment I fell in, I was engulfed. I knew I'd made a mistake, a really big mistake. I had never felt a current so strong. At 60 pounds soaking wet, it didn't take much to make for a strong current. Since I could touch the bottom, I tried bouncing myself above water. But the circular motion of the whirlpool made it impossible for me to stay up. I couldn't stay on top long enough to get a good breath. And I was taking in water faster than I could swallow. I was losing air. After taking my last gulps of muddy, cold water, what meager thoughts I was able to compose included the belief that I was done for. I was cooked. My throat was closed and nothing could get out or in. Ten paltry years was all I would get on this planet.

Suddenly, out of nowhere, just like in the movies, I felt a hand grab my shirt and effortlessly zip me out of the water. My head popped out as if I was a released flotation bob. I tried breathing, but desperate gasping was all I got.

"Mark, cough!" Someone was slapping me on the back. "Cough, Mark! Cough!"

The voice and arms belonged to Ion. He was one of the older kids in the village, and one of the biggest. At 16, he already had arms the size of tree trunks. He must've gotten them from his mom. She was a big-boned woman. We knew better than to tick her off. She once slapped one of our friends so hard for peeing on her gate that his neck hurt for a week.

I eventually got my air back. Ion had come out of nowhere and saved my life.

I had been both a rescuer and a *rescuee*.

Many years later, it seemed I may have been in need of rescue again. Initially, I felt insulted. How dare these people think of me depraved? But then I considered another possibility: if the Veljas and the

Gheorghes both wanted to rescue me, is it possible it might be for a good reason?

Was I a black sheep needing rescue? Was I sinking in a whirlpool of my own depravity? I thought I had already crossed over to the other side. Australia was supposed to fix *all* my problems, not create any.

What else was there?

One day, back in the Padinska Skela prison, I heard a group of guys singing in the corner of the large cell block. I suppose there was only so much blank staring and napping one can do before breaking out into song. I recognized the songs as gospel hymns I'd heard growing up.

"Hey, how do you guys know those songs?" I asked.

One of the older guys, Laurentiu, answered, "My mom is a Repenter. I grew up in a Repenter church. So did these guys." He pointed to the other men.

"So you're a Repenter, no?"

"Nah!" He waved his hand in a dismissive manner. "Not even close. I live like hell. But when I get to Australia I'm going to give my life to Jesus."

A few years later Laurentiu and I connected in Australia. He still ranted on about "giving my life to Jesus and stop living like hell." He had a teenage son he wanted to take care of. He wanted his son to know an upright Laurentiu. "But not today," he always added. "I just can't give my life to God today." Obviously, he had a few addictions he was afraid to give up.

"One day," Laurentiu kept saying.

One day Laurentiu went fishing with a friend. The two friends were fishing on top of different rocks. At one point his friend noticed Laurentiu was not responding anymore. He yelled at Laurentiu to jolt him awake. He even threw a stick to get his attention. Nothing. Laurentiu's friend pulled his line in and walked over. When he nudged him, Laurentiu tipped over lifelessly. He had no breath, no pulse.

Laurentiu died far too early. He died living like hell, never having given his life to Jesus, never allowing himself to be rescued. The intention was there. The action was not, proving the old proverb, "The road to hell is paved with good intentions."

One day.

Would I allow my *one day* to happen? Or would I vanish like Laurentiu, a lost sheep, carried by the current of the world from one temporary pleasure to another, never having reached the shore, never going beyond the *intention* of changing my life?

- - -

In May I turned 21. I was having lunch with Peter when I told him I was thinking of changing my life.

"How come?" he asked.

"I'm not sure if I'm such a good person. If something were to happen to me, I don't know where I'd go afterwards."

"You believe in Heaven?" Peter asked.

"Yes."

"Do you think changing the way you live will cause God to open up a spot in Heaven for you?"

"Sure. I think God wants me to be different. He probably wants me to be nicer, stop drinking and smoking and treat women differently," I told him.

"I think you're right about that. But even if you didn't smoke, and you looked at women differently, you'd still have lots of work to do."

"Like what?"

"You need to be perfect."

"Perfect?"

"Uh-huh."

"I can't do that. No one can!"

"Exactly! That's the whole point of surrendering to Jesus. He was the only perfect One. By surrendering to Him, it means God looks at Him instead of you when judgment time comes. You need to surrender your life so it can be rescued by Jesus. Do you remember the story you told me about the black lamb you rescued?"

I nodded.

"Imagine you are that black lamb. You're drenched and stuck. You know you need to get out of the water. That much is obvious. After all, that's what you're crying for. The problem is your circumstances are too much for you. You just don't have it in you to get out of your predicament. The only way you can escape your mess is if you cry out for someone to pull you out." He paused. "Mark, thinking and acting different is not what rescues you, what 'makes you saved.' *You can't save yourself.* No one can.

"This business about being different, this thing about being good, all so you can go to Heaven is typical empty religion. If God exists, and He's so huge, what sense does it make that you can actually earn enough to please Him? How can such a huge God be satisfied with your meager sacrifices?"

"What does God want then?"

"God wants all of you. He wants your life, not your bad habits. Being 'different' is a result of being rescued – you have become a different person. You develop an affection for your Rescuer that you didn't have before…because you didn't know Him. You are grateful for your rescue. You develop a relationship with your rescuer and now your outlook on life is different. A lot of people are afraid of surrendering their life to Jesus because they think God will take away all their fun.

But they have it all wrong. Certain things won't be fun when you have given your life to Jesus. You won't want to do them anymore. You won't get the same pleasure in some of the old things you used to do because you are now a new person.

"Mark," he said, "you need to repent of your sins, ask God for forgiveness, and then allow Jesus to be Lord of your life."

"So…I shouldn't try to be different?"

Peter shook his head. "Accept your need to be forgiven and saved. Listen carefully." He leaned in as if about to tell me a secret. "Only God, through Jesus Christ, has the power to save you. You do not have such power. The best thing you can do is acknowledge that you're at the mercy of God and ask Him to save you. Once you truly do that, the outward changes will follow. You become different as a result."

I sensed what Peter was telling me was true. But the closer I came to surrendering, the scarier the idea became. What would *surrender* mean for my life? Would I turn into some super, fanatical freak who peppers everything he says with hyper-religious words and sayings like "Lord willing" and "blessed this" and "blessed that?" Would I have to stop watching soccer because the players swear and have sex with many women? Would I have to stop talking to my co-workers because they weren't like me? Would I have one of those annoying, permanent smiles plastered on my face? And what if I couldn't live up to everyone's expectations of what a Christian is supposed to look like?

My roommates only reaffirmed my anxiety.

"You might have to quit smoking," Gaius said.

My other roommate chuckled. "Haven't you tried already?"

"Yeah, twice," I said, as I took a puff. "Come on guys! Let's be serious here. I think Peter may be right. Are you guys telling me you never felt this way? Like there is something more to God?"

"I really don't know what you're talking about. You're acting as if you're this terrible person and God hates you for it. That's why I don't go to that church anymore." Gaius had a disgusted look on his face. "All those people do is accuse you and make it seem like everything you do is bad. How can smoking and having a beer make you so terrible? How can it be bad to be with a woman when God gave us those urges? You go to work, pay your bills and stay out of trouble – now you're telling me you think you need to be saved? From what? You haven't killed anyone. You don't hurt people. God is love, right? If He loves you, what do you need to be saved *from*?"

I wanted to tell my roommates the part about needing to be perfect, but I didn't think they would understand.

A few days later, on a rainy Sunday morning, I was on our balcony, debating whether I should go to church. My roommates were sound asleep. I'd been up since the crack of dawn, watching the sun come up, sipping coffee and smoking cigarettes. I felt as if I was the only person awake. Maybe the lack of requests this early morning would allow God to focus a little more on my little dilemma. "Should I go to church or not?" No answer. I asked again. I'm not sure if I was expecting an audible answer. I was hoping that in whatever form the answer would arrive, I would understand it. I hoped I wasn't like the sheep that resisted being rescued.

At the last minute, I put on fresh clothes and went to church.

Pastor Gheorghe preached that morning. I was sitting on the left side, where the men usually sat. I don't remember the entire sermon or even its premise. But I vividly remember him mentioning man's need for repentance and accepting Jesus as his only possible means for salvation. It was all I needed to hear. I was ripe for the picking. A huge weight was pressing down onto my shoulders. It was an indescribable metaphysical pressure. All the intellectual battles ceased at that moment. I was sure God was urging me to take action.

It's decision time, Mark.

Scene after scene of things I had done throughout my life, things I knew God found detestable, scrolled across the screen of my mind. I started crying. The weight was crushing me. I was sitting on the second row from the front. No one else was crying.

God is real, I thought. He's been chasing me all this time. He preserved me in the river, He guided me in the dark, He shielded me in the barn, He directed my steps in the field, and now, He put His messengers in my life. He'd been pursuing me because I had been lost my whole life. It didn't matter that my dad was a pastor or that I used to sing in the church kids choir. I had always been lost.

I felt Him. I felt a deep remorse for living 21 years in selfish, self-imposed ignorance. I cried more, still the only one. My sobs carried through the small chapel, bouncing off the ceiling panels.

It's decision time, Mark.

Pastor Gheorghe asked if anyone wanted to give their life to Jesus. Without hesitation, I stepped out into the aisle, took a right turn, and knelt at the altar. I wanted to give my life to Jesus. A few men from the first pew came to pray with me. They put their hands on my shoulders. I now heard some ladies crying in the back.

I cried and prayed. I asked God to forgive me. I asked Jesus to be my Savior. The men agreed with me. They pleaded on my behalf. The weight was being lifted, as if every tear drop was carrying a portion of that burden off of me.

Isaiah's inquiry, "How long, Mark?" had finally been answered.

I had finally crossed over to the other side of the fence. I had found true freedom.

- - -

Smoking was always a huge no-no within Repenter circles. Their syllabus is, in many ways, akin to that of the American Puritans, especially concerning drinking and smoking. The common perception was that if you were smoking or drinking you were probably doing something else that was worse. And the assumers usually assumed you were doing the very worst of whatever bad things their overzealous, judgmental little hearts could imagine. Appearance counted for a lot. It was overemphasized. Refraining from smoking and drinking was one of the most visible ways of standing out in a communist society that forbade conventional evangelism.

But just because Repenters escaped a society that forbade evangelizing didn't mean they stopped perceiving smoking and casual drinking as the dividing line between Heaven and Hell.

I once heard someone offer a good illustration of how one can be both saved by Jesus *and* a smoker. "Imagine you are an onion," the man started. "Now imagine that first dead layer you usually peel off, the dry crusty part that you throw away, that's God peeling the death from you. That's salvation. What we now have is a usable, live onion, useful for nourishing. Your spirit has been brought to life. But the peeling has just begun.

"You have several other layers that God intends to peel off as He gets further down toward your spirit's core. Maybe there's some bitterness and anger He wants to rid you of. Perhaps there is past relational hurt you need to be set free of. Or anger. Possibly a propensity for lust. Layer after layer, God peels away. And somewhere in between, there may even be a smoking layer."

The initial reason for this illustration was sparked by someone who wanted to know if "his friend" really was saved, since he smoked. "You wake up one day, light one up as you accompany it with a cup of coffee and…all of a sudden you feel guilty! You start to feel pretty crummy about this smoking problem. 'What's going on here?' you ask. That, friend, is God saying, 'It's time to deal with *this* issue.'"

I enjoyed having my first cigarette of the day. I liked a cigarette after lunch. Smoking was a reason to take a break at work. And if I'd been working especially hard, that smoke was even better. There was also the quality time with my roommates. We were usually together in the afternoon. We spent a great deal of time on the balcony. We talked, knocked back a few cold ones and smoked. Our ashtray looked like a ravaged landscape with the butts hanging out like tree stubs. It just didn't feel right to sit around and talk without a cigarette dangling from the corner of your mouth. It was like having pork chops without a side. Who does that? Everyone knows you can't have pork chops without potatoes.

But God would not allow me to enjoy smoking anymore. It's time, He was saying. *We're dealing with this now.*

I went into my room and shut the door. I knelt and prayed. "Lord, you know me," I said. "You know I really want to get rid of this wretched cigarette. And you know I can't get rid of it by myself. I tried." I was weeping. "Please take this away from me. I don't want it anymore. It's holding me back."

Those were my words but I don't believe they were my thoughts. God was the one informing me my smoking habit was holding me back. From what in particular, I wouldn't know for a while.

I didn't say anything of my latest resolution to anyone. After three days the guys realized I wasn't showing up on the balcony anymore.

When they asked me why, I shrugged and said I didn't want to smoke anymore.

"Did the people at church say something to you?" someone asked.

"No. They didn't. I'm quitting because I think it's the right thing to do," I said.

"So, are we wrong for smoking?"

"That's between you and God," I said.

Ultimately, my roommates respected my decision. And from there on out, God continued to help me and I never smoked again.

- - -

Anna's mother, Christine's grandmother, had a vacant bungalow behind her home. She offered to rent it to Simon and me. Peter and Anna thought it a good idea that I move in with Simon. My current roommates may not have been the best influence for a new believer, they concluded.

The way I looked at it, moving there was advantageous in other ways. It may give me the opportunity to see Christine a little more, I reasoned. Judging by the split-second exchanges between us, I concluded Christine was a different type of girl. A *good* different. She seemed to know something other girls her age did not. She, however, would probably say nothing could've been further from the truth. Nevertheless, Christine had an air of seriousness that set her apart from other church girls. She inspired me. I liked her.

My new place was supposed to make it easier for me to be a believer. Not that being a believer would be easy.

I remember Peter saying, "Mark, once you give your life to Christ, you will see temptation like you've never seen before."

When Peter said this to me it meant very little. Growing up I had learned that everything was temptation. Feel like taking the neighbor's apples? That's temptation. Thinking of spying on your fellow church members? That's temptation. Do you ever just want to punch your classmates for making fun of you? Careful, that's temptation.

So when Peter wisely predicted the future, I hardly gave it a thought. I certainly wouldn't have seen temptation come the way it did.

There was a group of girls at church who, unbeknownst to me, were always in some form of competition over boys. During the next few years, I would learn this competition between young girls like this was normal.

There was a particular girl named Laura who made it obvious she was into me. Although I didn't completely reciprocate her feelings, I didn't exactly make it clear either. One day she invited me to hang out at her sister's apartment. The plan was to play board games and have dinner. This sounded innocent enough. After all, they were all nice, church-going people. What could go wrong?

I arrived at Laura's sister's apartment after work. Laura hugged me and offered a seat at the counter. The owners of the home welcomed me and asked if I'd like anything to snack on until dinner was ready. I told them I wasn't that hungry, the popcorn in front of me would do.

Ten minutes after my arrival something came up.

"Mark, I'm sorry, but we just got a call and have to leave," Laura's sister said.

"Is everything alright?" I asked.

"I think so. Family business. We'll know when we get there." She and her husband hurried out the door. And just like that, the owners of the home were gone and it was just Laura and me.

Laura asked me to move to the living room to watch television. We took turns switching the channel dial. We talked a little, but nothing of consequence. Just empty chit-chat. It was even awkward at times.

I never felt there was much substance to Laura. There was something careless, some form of immaturity I couldn't quite identify in her. The entire time at her sister's apartment I was thinking I should leave. But I didn't want to be rude. Laura was a nice girl and I'd have to see her again. I didn't want things to be weird between us.

It was my turn to turn the dial. I stepped across the room to the television. I bent down and started to turn the knob. *Click.* Nope. We're not watching that. *Click.* Nope. Not in the mood for the news. *Click.* "Hey! Look, it's *Sale of the Century*! I like this show!"

As I was finishing my thought, I turned around to walk back toward the couch. I was completely unprepared for what I saw. Laura was unzipping her pants, having already removed everything from the waist up.

"Hey, hey!" I said. "Wh—what are you doing?"

She stopped and looked at me, bewildered.

"I thought…I thought you…"

"Stop that, please." I blinked a few extra times.

"Sorry, Mark. I thought I could – maybe I could convince you."

"Laura, please put your clothes back on." I sighed. "I think I should leave."

It was strange how easy it was to walk away from the whole situation. To say *no* to Laura. After all, she was attractive. But I didn't want Laura.

I wanted a girl who, thus far, showed very little interest.

-8-

CHURCH GIRLS

Before escaping Romania I almost married a girl I was dating. But the entire time I was with her, I had a feeling I shouldn't be with her. The reason?

Church girls.

When I was little, my friends and I used to say that when we were ready to marry, we were going to marry church girls. Even in youth we knew church girls were the marrying type and the others were not. Surprisingly, my friends from later years in the city, none of whom had anything to do with any church, frequently mentioned their desire to marry church girls as well. After some time, we had plenty of fodder to know why church girls were the marrying type and the others – we called them *disco girls* – were not.

The girls I knew in Romania were destined to give me a life of troubles. There was always some ridiculous drama lurking around every corner. Someone was either sleeping with someone else's boyfriend or husband, or thought her boyfriend or husband was sleeping with someone else. And if no one was sleeping with anyone, that was also reason for concern. All this was added to their incessant bickering and gossip. It was as if they could only thrive on a constant diet of drama and emotional mutilation. The circus train never stopped. People jumped on and off, performing their tricks from car to car, never intending to take up a more suitable profession.

My girlfriend in Romania was not a church girl. She was a worldly girl. I was a worldly man. She thought we should marry. I didn't. Maybe I wasn't worldly enough. I wanted to get off the train.

A couple of years later I was no longer a worldly man. I wanted a godly woman. A church girl. I had just the one in mind.

In August of my first year in Australia, I called Christine Velja for the very first time. "Just to talk," as she later excitedly explained to her dad.

Christine was beautiful. I'd wanted to call her for some time. But for the first few months I was uneasy about doing so. Although she spoke Romanian better than I spoke English, I knew there would be a bit of a language barrier until I learned more English. But the larger reason for my hesitancy was because she was a church girl. Church girls were a little different, most of them anyway. But Christine, especially. I felt there was more to lose with Christine, as if I had one shot — one shot only — to not be ridiculous. So in August I eventually mustered up the courage to make a nonridiculous move. I was a new man. I understood her *Rom-glish* a little better and was no longer hiding cigarettes in my socks.

"You know," she said, "the very first time I talked to you, I looked down at your legs and could tell you were hiding cigarettes in your socks."

"How? The whole point of putting them there was so no one could see them."

"All you Romanian boys do that. Where did you ever get such *stew-ped* ideas?"

"From one another. Duh!"

She laughed, and then continued. "And if there was any doubt, that first Sunday Dad invited you over I could smell cigarette smoke on you. You weren't very clever, you know."

"I do know. A lot of things have changed since."

"I noticed," she said.

"You have?"

"…yes."

"What else have you noticed?"

"That's all."

After an hour of talking, I asked if I could call her again. She said I could. So I did. And later I called again. After a few chats, she told me her father and "mum" wanted to know if I'd come over for dinner. This time there would be very little interrogation of my spiritual state, she assured me. That report, they felt, was already in.

By the beginning of the next year I was a regular at the Velja home. I went over for dinner three to five nights a week. In the span of only five months, I'd practically become family. Anna cooked great meals, Peter had taken to mentoring me, and talking to Christine after dinner was a healthy, safe way for us to get to know each other. Eventually, Christine would reveal satisfactory details like how she noticed me the first day Toma Toma escorted the boys and me to the front pew of the Melbourne church. I knew it! I thought to myself. She told me the reason she may have seemed so cold at first was simple: I wasn't a believer. She knew that much immediately. "There's no point in getting to know a nonbeliever, no matter how good-looking or charming he may be," she explained.

"All I heard were good-looking and charming," I said.

"I wasn't talking about you," she said smiling and then straightening her face again.

For the most part, there was very little conventional dating between us. At first we didn't purposely avoid conventional dating (although we do both agree conventional dating is, for the most part, very flawed). Our lives were so crammed with activities that there was very little time for dating. Christine had piano and swimming lessons, a part-time job (which was her 16th birthday gift), school, and anytime the church doors were open, an expectation to be there. In the Velja home, you practically had to have a broken leg to miss church.

I also was working on a few things. Aside from the various jobs I would work over the next few years, I was elected to the church leadership team within a year of my arrival Down Under. It started out by being asked to lead various groups and undertake a variety of tasks, such as youth activities and group prayer. I found the church leaders exhibited a trust and faith in me I didn't even have in myself. Gheorghe and Peter were most instrumental in my being fully immersed in church work. "I see you more than just sitting in the pew," Peter once said.

"Me? Nah."

Although I dismissed their assertion at first, I eventually thought of it as more plausible as person after person reaffirmed Peter and Gheorghe's notion. I considered that God may indeed want me to go into ministry work. So I prayed about it. The concept of ministry was nowhere near foreign to me, considering my upbringing. My reservations may have had more to do with the politics I knew all too well to be deeply ingrained in church work. At times, I found it strange that someone as young as I was could be esteemed so highly, and so quickly. And it's not just that I was young (I was 22). I was an even younger believer (I was one). But I guess I wasn't perceived as young and unqualified as I really was. I had 14 years in the household of a preacher. That counted for something, I suppose.

On Easter of 1982, I was asked by Pastor Gheorghe to preach my first sermon. I realized after a few minutes of protest there was no point in doing so. I was going to do it. He knew it, and I knew it.

When I started the sermon, I was nervous. My hands trembled. My forehead grew hot. And every second that wasn't filled with the sound of my voice felt like I could park an entire episode of *Little House on the Prairie* in it. But I eventually lost myself and poured out what God put on my heart.

Considering Christine's busy schedule and my coming up through the ranks, we understood we were in the foundational stages of our lives. We never argued about the time we didn't spend together. Not even when my already busy schedule acquired another commitment.

In 1982, at the behest of Gheorghe and Peter, I enrolled at Victoria Bible College. During my time there, I grew exponentially. As a result, I began to take my work in ministry even more seriously. This may have been the exact period of time I became sure full-time ministry was what I was made to do. I became so convinced of my forthcoming place that the money-earning jobs became secondary, sometimes to the point of jeopardizing them.

By then, I was working at a radiator manufacturing company. The afternoon shift worked with my hectic schedule. I knew from the first day that sooner or later there was going to be trouble at the radiator factory.

Everyone had his own work station. The thing to do was to customize it. But it seemed my colleagues lacked creativity. All of them had some sort of poster, calendar or bulletin that displayed a naked woman, or a group of them, on their station wall. It was as if there was an unwritten decree, which stated all employees must contribute at least one display of nudity to the work environment. You could vary everything else about the decoration – the weather the nude woman was enduring, her posture, her facial expressions, the type of car she was blocking – but she had to be naked. And the nudity did not end with the work stations.

There were nude photos in the lunch room and on bulletin boards, as well. It was as if a truck stop and an adult magazine store came together and exploded in our factory.

I didn't get the memo. Nobody told me the rules. One day I decided I was going to do my own customizing. In my work station, on the large metal panel that was my wall, I started welding the letter *J*. This wasn't a small *J*. It was a big *J*, at least a foot, maybe two, in height, top to bottom. I stepped back and analyzed the big *J*. It needed to be a little thicker. So I went over it with my welder again. Then I stepped back to admire my work. It was good. On to the next letter. *E*. Then another one. *S*. And so on. *U. S.* then a space. I wasn't done. *I. S.* Now I had to go lower. I made the letters too big. I hunched over a little to get the last letters. *L-O-R-D*.

It was time to go home.

The next day, before starting my shift, I was pulled aside by the shift manager. "Mark, we need to talk," he said. He was wearing a serious look. He walked me to my station, as if I had forgotten the way. As we walked by, some of the men peered at us with giddy suspicion, putting very little effort in hiding their suspenseful delight. Once we got to my station, he looked at my wall. I followed suit. Yup, there it is. Just like I left it yesterday, I thought. JESUS IS LORD. It looks bigger than it did yesterday. It was so massive, so distracting. It might as well have been flashing in neon pink. JESUS IS LORD—flash—JESUS IS LORD—flash—JESUS IS LORD.

"Do you know anything about this?" Manager asked.

"About Jesus? Sure! What do you want to know?" I asked.

"No, no," he shook his head, rolling his eyes back. "What I meant is, did you write this?" He looked in pain, as if he wished he was not the manager at the time.

"Yes," I answered. "It's my work station."

"Why?"

"This is my work station." Maybe he was distracted by all the na-
kedness and didn't hear me the first time. "All these other guys have
their naked posters on their walls – well, this is who I am. That's who
they are," I pointed to a poster of naked girl on a motorcycle across the
aisle –"this is who I am." I pointed to my wall.

JESUS IS LORD.

He sighed and scratched the side of his head. "You have to take
it down."

"What do you mean?"

"You have to scrape it down." He put his hand on his hips and
tightened his lips.

"I'm not going to do that," I said.

"Mark, I'm warning you. If you don't scrape it down, you'll be
fired."

"It took me a long time to do that. I'm not going to take it down."

"Go home, Mark."

I went home.

At dinner I told the Veljas I'd been fired. Peter and Anna didn't
quite know what to make of it. Peter couldn't decide if I was being
juvenile or brave. Christine, at first, thought I was making the whole
thing up. When she concluded it was totally something I would do,
she was mostly proud of me. She had known about the naked posters
from day one. She thought the gang of men at the factory boorish and
childish. She had lightly remarked something about how one day my
stubbornness might get me in trouble. After three years of courtship, it
was precisely my stubbornness that would be the major building block
to the wall that would separate us.

Christine and I grew up in very different Repenter contexts. Although both outlooks may have been considered "fanatical" from certain perspectives, one was more "fanatical" than the other.

Although Dad had broken free from the Orthodox Church and found a freedom and casualness in the Repenter way of living (when compared to that of the former), the way believers lived in places like Bozovici was very strict compared to way Christians lived in the West. Anything that seemed remotely like a command in the New Testament was taken far more literally where I grew up. For instance, the Bible says a woman should not dress like a man, or vice versa. If you were a woman in Bozovici, you could never wear pants, even though there were pants made especially for women. As far as some were concerned, pants should forever remain a man thing.

It is also important to mention that most of these made up rules took a quite a bit of finagling to connect them to Biblical teachings. One of these rules said a preacher must wear a suit jacket whenever he's behind the pulpit. If you asked someone why some church leaders enforced such a made-up rule and passed it off as a command, they would probably jibber-jabber something about being "presentable" in the house of God, implying God was especially interested how you dressed in certain buildings.

Although I spent a great deal of my teenage years out of church, I still had 14 solid years in the strict Repenter church in Bozovici. The stringent rules and traditions were what I knew and associated with "real" Christianity. My fervent enforcement of the rules was also what gave me favor with the older generation in Australia, especially among the men who had insisted on my involvement in ministry. They reinforced my outlook. We were on the same team. And I was the just the promising rookie that the franchise needed. But I didn't have the person I wanted most on my team, Christine. It was proving more difficult than I anticipated. Christine was not one to change her ways without seriously assessing what she was asked to rethink. This characteristic was something I usually admired about her. But now it was proving a pain in my neck.

Our arguments were usually related to our differing views on spiritual matters. We argued over a gold-plated bracelet she wore to her older brother's wedding. In the Bible, Saint Peter talks about how a woman's beauty should not be merely outward. Then he mentions jewelry and braided hair as an example of "outward adornment." But it doesn't eliminate decorative appearance. The spirit of the text is that the essence of a woman's beauty should be in a godly character, not in a nice, outward appearance. However, me being the zealous and parochial Christian leader that I'd become, I brought the fallacy of her outward adornment to her attention. I pretty much told her she shouldn't wear the bracelet.

Christine thought my view on the bracelet completely asinine. And she let me know it. By that point, I'd already been contemplating whether Christine was capable of accepting my leadership as head of the relationship. Her defense was that few other young women had a better role model for submissiveness than she did. Although her mother "ran the home," she always let her husband set the course. Anna may have administered the bills and paperwork, but Peter brought home the paychecks and had final say on how the money would be spent. She may have made decisions regarding the children, but none without Peter's executive approval. Anna voiced her input and opinion, but should there be any divergence on an issue, Peter's final word became reality. Of course she was capable of being submissive, Christine reaffirmed me.

I was unconvinced. The way I saw it, Christine was repeatedly challenging me. I started to think this would lead to serious problems should we get married. And, yes, it was always clear to both of us that marriage was the aim; especially after three and a half years. Christine had even acknowledged her original future plans might have to be altered. Her initial plan – she revealed it during a chummy heart-spilling session – was to finish high school and college, and by 25, be married with at least one child. Despite the level of transparency that was her style, I clearly understood she was willing to concede ground on said plan; she made it clear, in a way only I'd interpret as clear, that she was open to being married before finishing college. I, on the other hand, made it clear, in a more direct manner, that being married to me would in no way minimize her chances of finishing college.

Our plans of marriage were discussed after three years of finally traversing a rickety, annoying bridge imposed by the very ones in our community.

When our church family found out we were together, they unanimously poked their noses into our lives and let us know that the whole thing stunk. The reason it stunk? They thought Christine wasn't Romanian enough for me. She was born in Australia, her mum came here when she was 17, and her dad was a Romanian born in Serbia. Christine was a counterfeit Romanian. The concept can only be fully comprehended if you're part of a certain ethnic group living in another culture. We were Romanians in an Australian society. And no one was prouder and more intent on keeping the *Romanian* part than the older generations, even if that meant imposing their worldview values onto others. And impose they did.

Gheorghe, along with many other people of the church, continuously suggested girls to me. They threw them at me like a deceptively sweet grandmother who insists you're only fooling yourself if you think you're fed enough. *How about this one? Or that one? Hey, Mark, I know the perfect girl for you.* They did it without shame, knowing full-well that I was courting and talking to Christine. In their defense, we never demonstrated our relationship in public. If you didn't have your ear to the ground, you wouldn't know Christine and I had dinner most nights. In public, we were two people who happened to go to the same church. But nevertheless, I felt we gave them plenty of evidence that we were together. Certain people we told flat-out that we were together.

There was an air of prideful ridiculousness in the vehement insistence to keep the Romanian community as Romanian as possible. The older generation, led by Gheorghe, simply didn't think Australians were as devout to being Christians as were Romanians. They perceived Australians as too loose in their behavior. Ironically, I'm sure there was a part of me who agreed with such a sentiment.

Christine's family had conformed to all the rules the church had written in invisible but staunch ink. Her mother and father sat on opposite sides of the aisle like everyone else; she didn't wear jewelry; she didn't wear pants, no matter how formal, to church. But none of that mattered. As far as our little church community was concerned, I needed a "real" Romanian girl to accompany me on the bright path that was my future in ministry. Christine would not do.

I begged to differ. The more I got to know Christine, the more I realized that she was exactly who I wanted *and* needed. She felt the same toward me. The mutual sentiment that we were meant to be together is how we got over our community's meddling in our relationship. By the time of the bracelet incident, Christine and I had also accepted that some people you just can't change, and we didn't so much care what they thought anymore. Some opponents even warmed up to the idea of the two of us together, perhaps only because they began to mind their own lives. Others, like Gheorghe and his wife, still held on to the hope that our relationship would crumble.

Now, it seemed their wish might become reality. We had this tiny problem of my stubbornness and Christine's refusal to adhere to its demands.

After intense arguing over my leadership, cosmetics, rules—made-up and otherwise—and that stupid bracelet, I suggested we take a break. Christine heartedly agreed. We were both very tired.

I went home, crushed. We had spent almost four years getting to know each other. For most of that time, I was sure Christine was the wife God intended for me.

Now what?

I wasn't ready to give up on something in which we'd invested so much. I wasn't ready to let Christine go. So I prayed, "Lord, if Christine is the woman you have made for me, have her call me. Then I'll know she's the one you have intended for me."

"If Christine ever calls me here, that's definitely God telling me she's the one," I said aloud.

Christine promised me she would never call me where I was staying at the time. I had moved out of Christine's grandmother's bungalow in order to live in one behind Gheorghe's house. There was no phone in my little abode. In order to receive a phone call, the caller would have to call Gheorghe's house. Someone in the house would have to walk over and notify me. Christine knew how Gheorghe and his wife felt about her, and she reciprocated those feelings in her own way. "Mark," she said, "I will neva—*eva*—call that house," when I told her where I was moving.

"Christine, it's a good opportunity to live by myself. I need the quiet," I explained. "It's impossible to study with Simon watching that blaring television all the time. And the rent will be cheaper."

"Okay, Mark. But don't expect a call from me."

Every day during our separation, I prayed about the woman I was supposed to marry, and whether or not that woman was Christine. Although I missed her and wanted to make sure she was alright, I didn't call her. I didn't visit the Velja home. I didn't write letters. I didn't drive by her house at night. I didn't hide in the bushes by her window. The only time I ever saw Christine was at church where we didn't say a word to each other.

Three months later, Mrs. Gheorghe, my landlord, knocked on my door. "Mark, are you there?" I heard.

My car was outside. She knew it was my day off.

"You have a phone call," she said.

"Who is it?" I asked, demurred.

"That Velja girl," she said.

Although the birds were chirping and it was a splendid Aussie day, I heard thunder clap and the sound of a whirlwind follow. *"Christine?"* I asked.

"That's the one."

"Are you sure?"

"Quite sure. I asked twice."

I put on my slippers, minded my rapidly beating heart and casually followed Mrs. Gheorghe to the main house, pretending there was nothing extraordinary about what was happening. My legs were quaking a bit, perhaps even trembling, as I almost tripped on flat surface.

The cream-colored receiver was lying on its side on the counter. It was waiting for me to receive it, to confirm three months of uncertainty. All I had to do was pick it up.

"Mark?" Mrs. Gheorghe looked at me bewildered. "Are you going to pick up the phone?"

I picked up the phone. "Hello?"

"Hey…"

I hadn't heard Christine's voice in ages. If I wouldn't hear it for another 50 years, it would still be as recognizable as it was that day. The sound of her voice would forever be ingrained in my mind. There was no else's like it. No other voice could be so fragile, yet sound so bold.

"Hey," I said, trying to sound normal.

"Can you pick me up from school?"

"Is everything alright?"

"I need a ride home. I want to discuss something with you. Can you come get me?"

"I can do that. I'll leave in a few minutes. I'll be there in an hour."

"Okay. You know where to find me." She hung up.

I did know where to find her. I was the one who dropped her off the first day of college. I also knew she didn't need a ride.

I was nervous. This was huge. My life was about to change. The test I'd put out confirmed this very thing. Could God have made it any clearer?

It was an amazing and equally unbelievable thing. God had answered me in exactly a manner I should have understood. Yet there was still a part of me that doubted God's voice with materialistic logic. Maybe this is just coincidence, I thought. People call people all the time, especially boyfriends and girlfriends. Even *ex*-boyfriends and girlfriends. They've been calling each other since the dawn of the telephone. So what if she called me here? Maybe it's coincidence.

Christine was standing under the pavilion, talking to another girl. I pulled around and stopped behind a line of cars. I was about to get out when she noticed me. I shut my door and reached across to make sure the passenger side was unlocked.

"Hey," she said as she slid in. She didn't smile. She turned around as she put her backpack on the backseat, not making eye contact.

"Hey," I said back.

I pulled around the car in the front. "How's school?" I asked.

"It's good. I think I'm really going to like being a teacher."

"You'll be good at it."

"Thank you."

I barely had the radio on. It helped with the awkwardness.

"Listen, I've been thinking and praying," Christine said, breaking the silence.

"Uh-huh."

"I've, well, I've been seeking God's will…" she stammered. "I've been seeking God's will and I really feel we need to get back together."

"What—"

"But I don't want to get back together just to continue the way we were," she continued, cutting me off.

I nodded. I couldn't have agreed more.

"We need to get married." She sighed. "Will you marry me?"

I turned my head, stunned. Although I hadn't expected that, I wasn't too surprised either. I kept my stoic composure. I couldn't let her take charge of our interaction.

"I'll think about it," I told her.

"Okay. Think about it. You have two days. You know where to find me."

I watched Christine walk up the driveway. I have the opportunity to spend the rest of my life with that woman, I whispered to myself. Will I let her walk away from me?

I don't think I had anything to think about. I'm pretty sure I had made up my mind two seconds after the question had left her mouth. I was being prideful. I really was stubborn.

The next evening, I called the Velja household. Christine picked up. She rarely answered the phone.

"Hey. It's me," I said.

"Hey."

"I made a decision. I need to talk to your dad first."

"Sure. We're all having dinner tomorrow night. Be here at seven. I'll set a place for you."

The next night there was a place for me. We made small talk before dinner. Nothing had changed. It was just like any other day I came over for dinner. I wasn't interrogated as to why I hadn't been over in three months or asked why I haven't been talking to their daughter.

After dinner I asked Peter if I could talk to him in private. He escorted me to the living room.

First, I explained a little of what had been happening between Christine and me, and why I hadn't been by. He listened patiently. I was sure he knew far more than I told him. He and Christine were very close.

"I want to talk to you about something serious," I said. He was sitting in his favorite chair.

"I'm listening." Like my own father, Peter possessed an innate sense of being in charge of an exchange even when someone else does most of the talking.

"I've been praying a lot – about your daughter and my future – together. I even put out a test to God. I believe God showed me that Christine is the woman He has prepared for me." I took a deep breath. "Peter, I'd like your blessing to marry Christine."

He didn't seem shocked. He was prepared to give an answer. "If it's God's plan, me and Anna approve and encourage your unity." He stretched out his hand and I shook it. Then we embraced.

Peter called Christine and Anna into the living room. He announced that he had given me permission to marry Christine. Anna whooped with excitement and embraced me. "Welcome to the family," she said into my ear.

"Now, Mark," Peter bellowed.

"Yes, sir?"

"You have to promise us something."

"What's that?" I asked.

"You have to promise me that you will refrain from giving us grandchildren until Christine is finished with school," Peter said halfway smiling. "Promise?"

I looked over and saw Christine blushing. No doubt the mention of pregnancy invoked mental images she probably preferred her parents not have.

"I promise," I said, smiling at Christine.

Christine told me later that once I had left that night, her dad had a word of caution for her. He wanted her to understand that marrying me would most likely mean anything but a completely private and settled life. Apparently, he knew my type well. I wasn't a pew warmer, I wasn't content with not growing and advancing; I was a go-getter, he informed her. That meant she was going to be right beside me, going and getting. There may be some scrutiny in her future, he wanted his daughter to know.

"Are you alright with that?" I wanted to know.

"It's not something I haven't already considered. Besides, I'm not too concerned with these details. If God has told me you're the one, then I expect He has taken all these things into consideration." I knew I picked a smart one.

The following Sunday, our engagement was announced at church. Christine said she noticed the instant shock in Gheorghe's face the moment the announcement registered.

During our six-month engagement Christine and I went to pre-marital counseling. I made sure to tell Christine everything there was to my past relationships. I even told her about the Laura incident that first year in Australia. I thought it important that there never be any surprises between us.

On January 5, 1985, Christine became Mrs. Christine Velja Hobafcovich and I became the husband of a beautiful, godly woman. A church girl.

-9-
DEDICATION

If I'm alone in the car at night, I don't normally listen to the radio. After a long day, I like peace and quiet. It helps clear my head.

I was going over the things a friend and I had discussed. We had unintentionally planted a little church in Brisbane, where I was studying in seminary. We started out as a Bible study group and, before I could take a second breath, I was pastoring Bethel Romanian Baptist Church. It wasn't unusual to meet with members well into the evening.

There was something soothing about the rushing night wind and the feel of muggy air blowing through one cracked-open window and exiting the other. I was cruising in my 10-year old beater under the star-filled, opaque outback country sky. Everything had wound down. The roads were empty. The shops were closed. It's was a fitting way to end the day, silence.

But this night was going to be different.

Just as I was reaching for the volume button, I heard something peculiar coming through the crackling speakers. The announcer grabbed my attention like a lazy hyena who'd just been jolted by the sound of injured prey: *"Nicolae Ceaușescu...fleeing...helicopter... government...caput...."* I couldn't make sense of it all. The static was not helping. I turned the volume up. *"Revolution...Romania...new government...."*

"What is going on?" I said out loud. "Is this for real?" I remember reading somewhere that when H.G Wells' *War of the Worlds* was broadcast on the radio in 1938, many people in America freaked out because they thought an alien invasion was actually happening.

Was I hearing fact or fiction?

I rushed home and practically forgot to unlock the door. In my rush to get to the television, I slammed into the locked door. Oops. I fumbled around for my keys until I finally barged through like a man who'd just barely escaped a violent pursuer wielding a sharp object.

"Christine, did you hear anything about—"

"Mark, what in the world is going on?"

Apron on, Christine was clutching the largest and sharpest kitchen knife we had in her right hand. "I thought someone was trying to break in!"

"I'm sorry. Is Hadassah sleeping?"

"For now!" She sighed. "If you wake her, you're putting her back to sleep."

Hadassah was our two-year old. We named her after Queen Esther, whose Jewish name was Hadassah. She was my little princess.

I quietly darted across the room and turned the television on. *Click...click click.* We still had an old style television. I finally found the news channel. The images showed rioting in Timişoara. That's where the trouble started, the news reporter explained. Christine had put the knife back in the drawer and was watching next to me.

After four decades of Communist rule, Romanians had revolted and were now in the middle of overthrowing their government. The footage depicted a war zone in a city I was very familiar with, Timişoara.

I don't think I slept for three days. I was preoccupied with reaching my two sisters, Petra and Chivuţa, who lived in Timişoara. I called several times, but couldn't reach either of them.

So I called Mary, hoping she may have spoken to someone in Romania. Mary was easy to contact. By this time, she was living in America. She'd been there for a few years. I helped her get there.

Before leaving, Mary went back and forth with the Romanian government for almost two years as she tried to convince someone to allow her to visit Australia. She wanted to visit her baby brother, she pleaded. They simply told her, "No." A lot. And if they didn't say *no* it was because they didn't respond. What else they were thinking I could only imagine. I'm sure at some point they put the pieces together — her brother illegally fled the country — and probably laughed at the gutsiness of my sister. *Gutsy* was probably an insufficient word. Mary was so determined to be allowed to see her traitor brother that she even wrote Ceaușescu himself asking for permission. I don't know what else she did, but I do know she eventually got permission to visit me in Australia.

When it was time for her to go back, I bought Mary an extra ticket. She had two tickets now: the ticket that went from Australia to Serbia and then on to Bucharest; and the second ticket that went from Australia to Belgrade to Vienna. Once in Serbia, Mary boarded the plane to Vienna instead of Bucharest. After four weeks of hanging around Vienna and waiting on her application for political asylum in the U.S. to be approved, Mary took a plane that brought her to O'Hare International Airport. She settled not too far down the road from Chicago.

Mary eventually got in touch with my sisters in Timișoara. "Don't worry, everyone is fine," she told me. I also learned that Dad, being the inquisitive man he was, actually took a bus to Timișoara "just to see what's going on." He heard "something" was happening and wanted to see for himself. The bus dropped him a few miles from Opera Square, which would later be renamed Victory Square, as a good bit of the fighting was done there. Dad was in the middle of a war zone. The city was littered with tanks and soldiers firing automatic rifles. Young people were shouting and throwing Molotov cocktails at the tanks and machine gun-toting soldiers. Women and children were screaming from balconies.

Dad had done his time in the army, but this was something he'd never seen. He wasn't going to make it to my sisters' apartments. After ducking and hiding behind solid objects to avoid being shot, he turned back to find a bus that would take him back to Bozovici, where the birds still sang and daisies swayed unbothered.

The revolution was all we talked about for weeks. Many of our Romanian friends in Australia, especially the ones who had lived in Romania as adults, wondered how the revolution could've started.

"There had to have been intervention of some sort," a friend suggested. "There is no way the next generation just woke up one day and decided to overthrow the government. Who knows how many years of planning it took?"

"I certainly never came across anyone who was part of any plans to revolt," I said.

"That's the thing. The system was just so cemented – communism was so ingrained. I never knew anyone either that so much as *whispered* a word about overthrowing the government. All the talk was about getting out."

My quiet friend then suggested that "it was the Russians."

"*The Russians?*" We were all listening.

"Ceaușescu just paid off the country's debt. Think about that – including the money owed to the Russians. That's the reason we all left. He was squeezing the country more than usual. You remember. No meat on the shelves; the electricity going out for days without any real reasons; farmers being robbed of more than ever before. It was all going to pay the debt."

"Wait a minute now!" I cut in. "What about the palaces he was building in Bucharest? What did that have to do with the debt? The man was building mansions with gold toilets for him and his friends with the money from our exports. The only thing you could consistently find in the market was pig's feet!"

"Yeah, it's true. It fits with the megalomaniac he was. He wasn't going to sacrifice any of *his* luxury. But he had no problem starving his own people while trying to make it seem like he was in control. He wanted everyone in the world to know he was his own man, not a pawn of anyone else, especially the Russians. Well, the Russians must not have liked that. Since he was no longer cooperating with them, they took him out. They instigated the riots by placing their KGB agents in the squares as disrupters."

"I think you guys are too hard on the man. What about the apartments he built so poor people in the country could live in the city?" someone else said.

"Let me tell you about those apartments. I got a letter from my parents a few years back. They told me they were ordered to move into one of those new apartments Ceaușescu built. They were excited at first. They always wanted to live in the city. After they moved in, the first thing they noticed was how small and poorly constructed their place was. The walls were so thin that you could make out the words of the conversation your neighbors were having."

"Maybe that was on purpose."

"And get this: there was no indoor bathroom!"

Someone laughed.

"There were outhouses behind the complex. An apartment complex with outhouses! Can you believe that? How's that for a compassionate leader?"

"Where did you hear about the Russian plot?" I asked.

"Do you know how many Romanians are here on political asylum?"

"If this was instigated by the Russians, that means they will have some say in who comes to power, right?"

"I'm sure. You watch who becomes the next president of Romania. If what I'm saying is *close* to true, I guarantee it'll be someone in the old Communist party."

I didn't know what to make of the speculation. To this day I'm not sure of what exactly happened. What I do know is in December 1989 Romanians overthrew their government. They killed Ceaușescu and his wife by firing squad on Christmas Day. It was broadcast on national television.

Merry Christmas, Romania.

- - -

We moved back to our home church in Melbourne, where we built our first home. We'd been back nine months when I got the phone call.

"Hello, this is Gordon Donahoe. I'm a pastor in Nashville, Tennessee. I'm looking for Mr. Mark Hoba...Hobayfcoevich — is Mark there?" There was a twang to the man's accent I'd only heard in John Wayne movies.

It was one o'clock in the morning. Had this American cowboy even considered that? My second-born, three-year-old Elizabeth, was awakened by the ringing and started crying.

"Speaking," I answered. "Mr. Donahoe, was it?"

"Yes. That's right. May I have a moment of your time, Sir?"

Why not? I was already awake. "How may I help you?"

"Mark, we are looking to plant a church here in Nashville. Do you know anything about Nashville?" he asked.

"Country music city?" I owned an encyclopedia. I stumbled on *Nashville* a while back. In class we were discussing the settlers' attempts to convert the Native Americans. Naturally, I wanted to know more about the Native Americans, but not before I would know something about Nashville.

"That's the one! Country music city, home of Opryland," Mr. Donahoe exclaimed, with a heavy drawl on the *mew* in music. "Anyway, I have been put in charge of helping to start a Romanian church here. There are a few Romanian families here and they need a shepherd. The problem is, we can't seem to find the right pastor to lead this small flock. We had an older fella' try, but it didn't work out so well. I was told about you by some dear Romanian friends of ours who know some people in Melbourne. They said you were young, bilingual, and a very nice man – exactly what we're looking for. Does that sound about right, Mr. Mark?"

"I'll take it, the compliment that is. Are you suggesting what I think you are?"

I could hear Christine whispering from the bedroom, wanting to know who was on the phone.

"Yes. We would like you to help plant a Romanian church here in Nashville," he continued. "We want you to pastor the church. We heard you and your family already have visas. What do you say?"

"Do I want to move to Nashville, Tennessee? Christine?"

A few years earlier, around Christmas 1988, Christine and I had visited Mary in Chicago. During our time in the U.S. Mary had arranged for us to visit an immigration lawyer. She wanted my family and me to move to the U.S. Although I was surprised that Mary did such a thing, I was not completely opposed to the idea. Christine, on the other hand, was not crazy about the idea, to say the least.

"This country is flooded with missionaries and pastors. Why would they need us here?" she said.

"I don't know. There probably is no need for me to be here. Let's first apply for residency, just to see what happens," I said. "If it's God's plan for us to move here, I think it will be made clear."

This eased Christine a bit, enough to convince her it would be harmless to apply. She was even more at ease after the initial interview. The application, we were told, will take awhile, even years. Especially since there was no actual job offer, business venture, or study plans. She definitely had nothing to worry about.

By the time we had moved back to Melbourne from Brisbane in 1992, we received a notice telling us we had arrived at our final step in the application process. We just needed to have an interview with the American consulate in Sydney.

Christine was shocked. We both thought the whole thing had been dead twice over by now. It had been four years! We had even bought a house.

So now with Mr. Donahoe's offer before us, I had to figure something out. Leaving for the U.S. was quickly becoming a reality...and a nightmare for Christine. It's not the way I wanted things to go. The last thing I wanted to do was drag my wife across the globe kicking and screaming and then to have her resent me the rest of our lives. That wasn't the type of thing that makes for a good marriage.

My in-laws were not pleased with the idea, either. "*America?!* Why America? They have thousands of churches – bundles and bundles of pastors. We need you *here*! And we don't want you to move away. We want to see our grandchildren grow up. You're not going anywhere. We're going to ask God to stomp this entire thing out."

I felt like a jerk. Anna and Peter didn't say as much, but I got the feeling they may have suspected one of the ulterior motives for my wanting to move to the U.S. had to do with my family. Not only were Mary and her husband and children living there, but after the revolution, my parents had moved to Chicago as well. I tried to make it clear as day, without accusing my wonderful in-laws, that my family was not my motivation for wanting to move to the U.S.

"Peter, I understand you may think my family is the reason I'm considering moving to America, but I can assure you my parents being in America have nothing to do with this decision. I've been without them for the last 12 years. I'm a big boy. I have my own family…and no one else comes before them. Christine is my family. Hadassah is my family. Elizabeth is my family. You and Anna are my family. Really, I don't even *want* to go to America. I told you that. If it were solely up to me, I wouldn't consider moving there for another minute. I mean it. It's just that, well, I think there may be something to this. And I don't want to be disobedient to God."

The next day I called the American Consulate in Sydney. I told them I wasn't sure if what I was doing was normal protocol, but I wanted to postpone the interview for exactly one year. "Can I do that?" I asked.

"Umm…really? You want to postpone? It says here you applied almost four years ago."

"Yes, that's correct. There are some things I need to work out. I would much appreciate one more year. We will be ready for the interview then. I promise."

"You can postpone, Mr. Hobaf – sir. It's a little unusual, but it can be done," the man said.

I had a year. We had a year.

Meanwhile, Christine and I were praying for guidance. We asked God to close any doors we weren't meant to go through and open those we were.

A year went by and we were called for the final interview. To Christine's shock and devastation, we were approved for permanent resident visas in the United States. No job, no real prospects – it didn't matter. That door was swung off its hinges.

We had four months to leave Australia.

Christine and her parents were dumbfounded. Their nightmare had become reality, and now, a great burden for me. Their misery was all on me now.

After a string of sleepless nights, I made the decision that we wouldn't leave. Plain and simple. Despite the door opening, there was no way I could do this to my family. I wasn't going to live the rest of my life with a cloud of resentment hanging over me. I told Christine we're not leaving.

"We're not?"

"No. This is not how I want it to happen."

Once the surprise wore off, she was relieved. But it wouldn't last. Something happened.

Since we would be staying in Australia, Christine applied for a teaching job at the school she grew up in. She was sure to get this job. She had all the credentials, certainly the references, and the connections to go with it. There was no way they would turn her down for the job. "There's no way," I agreed.

She didn't get the job. She told me that since I told her we wouldn't be leaving for the U.S. she'd been in turmoil. She said she prayed for one last sign: whether or not she got the teaching job. That would be the obvious answer. She now knew and accepted that we must be obedient and move to the U.S.

We told the Veljas of the more recent developments. "We changed our minds…again. We're going to the U.S.," I said.

Their reaction was miraculous. Like Christine, they now also understood this is what had to happen. "We see it now," Peter said. "I want you guys to know that you go with our full support and blessing."

"But you better visit – and visit often," Anna added. "I want to see my grandchildren."

We had three months to sell the house and get out of Australia. Selling the house seemed an insurmountable obstacle. Even though the market was solid, it was very rare to sell a house in three months. And secondly, where in the U.S. were we going? It's a massive country. Outside of my family, we didn't have any contact with anyone there.

That's when Mr. Donahoe from Nashville, Tennessee called.

I shuffled back to the bedroom. Christine was walking back and forth with Elizabeth in her arms. "What was that about?" she asked.

"That was the American pastor. I think he just asked me to pastor a church in Nashville."

"Country music Nashville?"

"That's the one. He somehow heard we had already been approved for visas."

"What did you tell him?" Christine asked.

"I told him I don't like country music. It's not my style."

"Nashville. How about that? Why not?"

"He'll be expecting our answer in a few days."

My wife and I knew this was the answer to our prayers. We were going to Nashville. And if there was any speck of doubt left over as to whether we should leave, it was gone when our house been sold a few weeks later.

Some of the church leaders weren't very happy about our departure. Gheorghe even asked from the pulpit why we were leaving. I smiled and chuckled, a little uneasy.

The church in Melbourne played a vital role in my spiritual development. They sent out Toma Toma to do a simple task and the man had done his duty flawlessly. The people in Melbourne fed me. Guys like Simon found my first job. He drove me to work until I could make my own way. The church leaders saw my potential and helped nourish it every way they could: they encouraged me to speak; they helped me go to school; and they honored me with a leadership role, one not to be taken lightly.

I easily forgave them for not coming to terms with my departure. They were people, only human. In this instance they reserved the right to be stubborn. It was their way of saying, "We will miss you and we love you."

- - -

We landed in Chicago in July 1993. It was hot. It was sticky. This day there was no sign of that famous wind so synonymous with the city. Another thing I noticed, which I may have overlooked on my visit years ago, was how dirty the city was. Trash littered the sidewalks, and when a gust of wind mercifully interrupted the sauna-like atmosphere, it gave elevation to the lighter of trash blowing it back and forth through the air.

Mary and her husband picked us up. They weaved their jam-packed car through the jam-packed city until we arrived at their home, a quaint 10th-story apartment.

"Tomorrow we're going to see Mamica and Tăticu. I can't wait to see their faces." Her eyes were wide and her smile wide. "Are you nervous?"

"No."

"I was talking to Christine."

"A little bit," Christine answered.

- - -

I awoke before everyone else, the sun still shy of peeking through. I don't think I slept at all. I'd spent the night on the couch, in the in-between state of half-awake, half-not. Everyone else was sound asleep. I stepped onto the balcony. It was going to be another muggy day. As far as I could see, it was building after building in every direction; tall and thin, wide and shorter. Some were grimy, others clean. Somewhere in this city of hundreds of buildings and millions of God-created breathing human beings were my parents. What a perplexing, amazing thing life is, I thought. For the longest time I'd come to terms that I might never see them again. And they may have come to the same conclusion about me. But now, we were just hours from reuniting. Not in Bozovici, not in Reşiţa, not even in Melbourne, but in a country where we were all strangers. And not just strangers to the country, but after all this time, strangers to each other.

I was growing nervous as the elevator slowly climbed the 16 stories. I was far more nervous by the time we cornered the shadowy halls, knowing I was only doors away.

"This is it," Mary said. It was a door like all the others. The rustic number on it said *1920*. I made sure my polo was tucked nicely into my jeans. I looked back and saw Christine adjusting her dress sleeve with her free hand.

"Go ahead." Mary insisted I do the knocking.

Knock, knock.

A chain jangled noisily on the other side. The knob turned, at first unsure of which way it should go. The door jolted loose and creaked as it slowly began swinging open. An old man with thick, graying hair appeared as the door incrementally retreated. Behind the wrinkles and under the discolored hair, I knew the man.

"Ohhhhhh ! *Doamne bun!*" he groaned, smiling from ear to ear.

"Hello Dad. Do you remember me?"

For a few seconds he just stood there smiling, perhaps reassuring himself he was not dreaming. He eventually embraced Elizabeth and me – Elizabeth was in my arms – in the doorway. Christine stood beside me, holding Hadassah's hand. Mary suggested we move inside.

"Elena, look who it is," Dad said, pointing to us.

Mom was behind him, crying.

"It's okay, Mom," I said. I walked over and hugged her. She tried to speak, but all she could do was nod her head and fight to keep her eyes open and dry.

"And who is this?" she asked.

"Mom, this is Christine."

"Hello, Mamica, Tăticu." She embraced Mom first, then Dad, each giving her a kiss on the cheek in return.

"And these two beauties...wherever did you find them?" Mom asked.

"That's Hadassah, and this is Elizabeth," I said.

"Hi!" Elizabeth spouted. Hadassah looked at them suspiciously.

"Hi, hi," Dad said. "I'm your grandpa."

"Hi *Bunicu*," she said back. "*Eu sunt* 'Lizbeth."

"Oh, Mark. She knows Romanian."

"Of course she does."

We gathered around the worn sofa and loveseat combo across from the television in their tiny apartment. The scent of lamb filled the room. Mom had been working on dinner. There was a butcher shop within walking distance. Everything was within walking distance, which was perfect for my parents. They weren't even going to attempt to learn to drive at their age.

Adult dinner conversation naturally turned to the old country. The best thing about the fall of the old regime, Dad said, was that he and Mom finally got their pensions. Because of my defecting, they were refused their retirement. That wasn't all.

"Sometime after Petra told us she talked to you, we had a visit from a government official," Dad said. "'Mr. Hobafcovich, do you happen to know where your son is?' they asked me. I said, 'No. Do you?' He wasn't convinced. 'Are you sure?' 'I wish I knew,' I told him. 'We have reason to believe he fled the country. Did he ever discuss fleeing the country with you?' 'No. He was working and living in the city. I rarely saw him,' I told them. A few weeks later I was 'laid off' from the depository, your mother from the office, and we found ourselves living off selling fruits and vegetables. It was obvious we weren't going to get our pensions."

"Dad you never told me this. Maybe I could've found a way to send you some money."

"How was I going to tell you? You know you can't talk about this stuff over the phone, or risk having your letters read." He took in a spoonful of garlic potatoes.

"Mark, God was good. He preserved us. Don't worry too much," Mom said.

After finishing dinner, I took a stack of dishes to the sink. Mom had already gotten started. Her eyes were glassy with tears.

"Mom, are you okay?" I asked.

"I'm good. I'm just really happy," she said, trying not to look at me.

Just as I was about to walk back to the living area with the others, she grabbed my arm. "I can't believe this day has come." She sniffed. "Last time I saw you, you were a very different person."

"I hope so," I said. I looked over my shoulder and saw Dad and Christine talking on the couch, and my daughters playing on the floor.

Mom had stopped stacking dishes. "You were an anxious boy who didn't know what he was doing. You didn't know what you wanted. But I got the feeling you knew that whatever you were looking for, you hadn't found yet. That much you knew. And you were a heathen." She smiled. "That I'm sure you didn't know."

"Yes, I was." I smiled back. "And no, I didn't."

"I knew you were, Mark. I knew you were doing things you knew better than to do, things we taught you not to do. And I prayed for you. I prayed a lot. Because I knew you were meant for more."

"Thanks, Mom."

"No, you don't understand, John Mark."

I'd never heard her call me by my full name. Despite 12 years without seeing her, I knew when my mom was holding something back.

"Look at you now. A grown man with a wonderful family, doing what you were made to do. That was always your special destiny. It was my promise to God."

"What was?"

"You are the result of prayer and a special dedication."

"Special dedication?"

Then she told me.

"The night you were born I was alone with Chivuţa. She was barely three. Everyone else was gone. I was cleaning around the house when my water broke. I fell on the kitchen floor. The dishes in my hands shattered everywhere. I'd had three children by then. I knew that pain well. I knew what was coming: *you*. I screamed in between contractions. Maybe I could get the attention of the neighbors. I needed someone. But no one heard me. No one came. I was in so much pain. 'Please, Lord, bring someone to me to deliver this baby,' I said. But still, no one came. It was just me and your sister. She was crying in the corner. She kept saying, 'Mommy, don't cry! Tăticu will be home. Stop crying!'

"I managed to finally give birth to you. The floor was a mess. And still no one came. I thought something happened and they were never coming back. After some time I was convinced I was going to die. I had a deep knowing that me and you were going to die right there on that floor. I had no doubt. Out of desperation I said to the Lord, 'God, if you let this boy and I live, I promise I will dedicate him to you.'"

She tilted up her soaked eyes, tears streaming down both cheeks.

"I asked your sister for a pair of scissors. She just kept crying. So I said, 'Chivuţa, sweetheart, if you don't get mommy a pair of scissors I won't let you wear that dress I made you for Easter.' So she brought me the scissors and I was able to cut the umbilical cord."

"Why did you wait so long to tell me this?"

All the background noise dissolved as I looked at my mom.

"You weren't ready for it. You were either too young, or a heathen, remember? Mark, you are the answer to a prayer. You are the result of my dedicating you to the Lord. All those years you strayed, God never stopped pursuing you. The way you escaped, the fire in the barn, the guard with the warning light – all those events you just told us about. Mark, that was the hand of God on your life. He shielded you from harm because I dedicated you to Him. He had special work for you the moment you were born."

I cried with my mom.

BIG PICTURE (EPILOGUE)

I don't know where Genu, Nick, Lucian and Johnny are today. I got together with a couple of them not too long after we separated at the hostel in Australia. But I lost contact shortly afterwards. Living a continent away has made the prospect of connecting with the guys more difficult. I hope a good deal of the rumors were not true, especially the one that involves incarceration.

I would definitely like to sit down and reunite with the guys. We could reminisce over our time in Romania, and even our escape. They could catch me up on their lives. And I could tell them about mine. I would love to tell them about my passion, the thing that keeps me going, that which inspires me to wake up each morning and live to the fullest.

One thing consumes me more than anything.

My good friend, Robby, knew a friend who was moving from Nashville to Atlanta. He asked if I would help him deliver a piece of furniture to her new apartment. I was living in the metro Atlanta area, and like any good Southerner, I had a truck. So, naturally, I was a good candidate for helping someone move.

I met with Robby and his friend, Rebekah. Rebekah's friend and soon-to-be roommate, Leslie, was also there. Robby and I picked up the mattress and delivered it to Rebekah and Leslie's apartment outside the perimeter. On our way back to their apartment, I asked Robby to invite the girls over for lunch sometime. He did and the girls accepted.

The following Sunday, Rebekah and Leslie came over for lunch after church. Christine had prepared soup, pork chops, and steamed vegetables. I bought a freshly-made tiramisu for dessert. We ate, we talked, then we ate some more. The girls complimented the meal as I fished for compliments on the dessert.

As we finished off the delicious tiramisu we transitioned to the topic of making disciples. The topic of baptism came up shortly after. We discussed how baptism didn't make one a believer, but that it was a commandment we should obey to the best of our ability. That's when Rebekah said she had never been baptized.

"Tell me more," I said.

"Umm...I don't know. Growing up, I didn't know Jesus. Going to church, or anything like that, was not something we did in my family. Once I got older, I accepted Jesus as my Lord and Savior. I was saved, but it never hit me that I never was baptized. I've totally overlooked it." Rebekah shrugged her shoulders.

"What are you going to do about it?" I asked.

"Well...I want to be baptized."

"That's good. When?"

She looked around for a second and said," Now...?"

"*Now?*" Robby and I asked.

"Sure."

"You mean *now* as in *now, now*? Or *now* as in whenever *now* comes?" I asked.

"Now as in right now. Now, *now*. You're a preacher. You can do it, right?" she asked.

"Yes, I am, but any Christian can baptize you. How to do you think the first century church in Antioch exploded? Remember, Stephen was martyred and the apostles fled and worked in other areas. But the church grew and people were being baptized. Besides, the Great Commission commands that you make disciples *and* baptize. Nowhere does it distinguish that you must be a special kind of Christian to do the baptizing part. Robby here can baptize you, "I said, pointing to Robby.

"I could. But I'll let Mark do it," Robby said.

"Okay," Rebekah said. "I want to be baptized...*now*."

As I was thinking about which bath tub was the bigger, Rebekah's friend told us she had never been baptized either.

"Really?" Christine asked.

"I've always known about it. I grew up watching people getting baptized. I guess I never saw it as a priority," Leslie said.

I said to Christine, "It looks like we're having a baptism. Now."

She smiled. "Let's do it. I have to find them something to wear."

A few months back, a man from the Central African Republic gave a friend two traditional floral African dresses. My friend, in turn, asked if I'd like the dresses, seeing as I had two daughters. I accepted the dresses, doubting my daughters would ever wear them. The traditional floral African dresses had been hanging on Christine's closet door.

I said, "Christine, remember the African dresses?"

She was already ahead of me. "I'm going to get them."

"You have African dresses?" Robby asked.

"Don't you?"

We filled the tub halfway with lukewarm water. Rebekah, dressed in the green and yellow African dress, stepped in. She then lowered herself in the water and settled on her shins.

"Rebekah, are you now trusting in Jesus Christ alone for the forgiveness of your sins and the promise of eternal life?" I asked.

"Yes, I am."

"Rebekah, do you intend with God's help, to obey Jesus' teaching and follow Him as your Lord?"

188

"Yes, I do."

"On the profession of your faith in Jesus Christ as your Lord and Savior, and in obedience to His command, I now baptize you in the name of the Father, and of the Son, and of the Holy Spirit."

Rebekah grabbed her nose and I dunked her backwards, then brought her back up.

"Congratulations," I said.

Christine wrapped Rebekah in a towel as she hugged her.

Leslie stepped into the tub next.

"Leslie, are you trusting in Jesus Christ alone for the forgiveness of your sins and the promise of eternal life?"

- - -

I am largely a result of one man, Toma Toma, being obedient to a simple task. He wasn't a preacher, a charismatic orator, or a brilliant teacher. He wasn't a licensed preacher. He was just a simple man being obedient. Where Toma Toma left off, Simon picked up. And so forth.

"What happens when you take making disciples and baptizing them seriously?" a friend once asked.

This is what keeps me awake at night.

This is what consumes me: making followers of Jesus and inspiring others to do the same. It's my mission. That's the last thing Jesus commanded before physically leaving Earth:

"Go and make disciples of all nations, baptizing them in the name of the Father and of the Son and of the Holy Spirit" *(Matthew 28:19).*

I am ultimately blessed to not only have the support of my wife and daughters in such work, but their obedience to the command as well. They're fellow workers. When Hadassah was younger, she befriended a neighborhood girl. For whatever reason, I found this young lady in our home a good deal. I think at one point I even asked Hadassah if she had moved her friend in without telling us. Over time, no doubt thanks to God working through Hadassah's persistence and friendship, her friend accepted Jesus Christ.

Elizabeth is involved in a ministry specifically dedicated to making disciples. She rearranged her entire life and moved away for the purpose of focusing on such work in a city desperately needing the power of the Gospel.

And as for Christine, I'm not even sure where to start. Christine was once recognized in a magazine for preventing a young lady from making a huge mistake – aborting her baby. She is feverishly dedicated to mentoring and teaching young ladies how to become godly women.

A Christian's calling, once he is matured, is to bring others to Christ and teach obedience to Christ. He is then to help new Christians develop into deployable disciples, so they in turn can do that which was done with them. The idea that you need to be a certain kind of somebody with a certain kind of skill to make disciples is wholly unbiblical. No greater lie could have been told to the Church. No one is exempt from the command of making followers of Christ. Perhaps because of the professionalism of our programs and leaders, especially here in the West, we have come to believe that adding to the church is specific work for the slick orator and entertaining, professional service leaders. I'll say it again: *nothing can be further from the truth*. As I heard a pastor once say, "This is not what it's about [being in church]. This is just the coach saying, 'Go and get them, team!' The work is out there. And you're the workers!"

Everyone is called to do the work, from the assembly line worker believer to the fast food cashier believer, to the high-powered CEO believer.

Making disciples is not easy. It'll cost you. First, it will cost you time. If nothing else, your time will have to be spent on people. Secondly, it will probably cost you money. Whether it be taking a mission trip, or sitting down for coffee or lunch with someone, you will most likely have to expend resources and time. Lastly, making disciples may even cost you part of your reputation. You may be asked to mentor or talk to certain characters that your community has deemed social lepers, hopeless or just plain shady.

Ultimately, making disciples means death to self. It means listening to God and being obedient. Even when it may look like there is no hope.

As it did with Julian.

As wonderful as spending time with Julian was, my ultimate goal when spending time with any unbeliever is to help secure his or her spot in a glorious eternity. I have accepted that not everyone I will invest in will come to the realization of Jesus as Lord and Savior. But I have found that when I persist in being obedient, amazing things can happen. God shows up.

Julian and his family were friends of friends. We met at one of our frequent weekend soirées in Brisbane. He and I took to each other.

Somewhere in our initial conversation, I revealed that I was in seminary, training to be a pastor. At first, Julian seemed unaffected by my professed goal. But afterwards, whenever we'd see each other, he'd jokingly greet me with one of a few monikers he had assigned me: Apostle Mark, Father Mark, Pope Mark, or, the name he was proudest of, Righteous Brother Mark H. "How's the Lord feeling today, father?" he once asked. Another time he asked if I ever thought about editing my Gospel so it may get as much attention as John's or Matthew's.

"Hey, Julian!" I said one day. "Why don't we talk about that?"

"About editing the Gospel of Mark?"

"Sure," I said.

He laughed and agreed.

As the kids were running in the grass, the other men grilling, and our wives having their own conversations, Julian and I engaged in the type of back and forth dialogue which would become routine.

"So, Julian? What's the deal? Why are you so stuck on my being in seminary?" I asked him.

He took a chug of his beer. "I don't know. I guess I find it interesting, that's all."

"Me too. That's why I'm doing it." I sipped my water.

"I don't think we find it interesting in the same way."

"Oh…?"

"You find it interesting because you assume it to be true, right?" he asked.

I nodded.

"I find it interesting that you assume it to be true."

"It?" I asked.

"It. He. God. The Great Big Guy in the Sky. The Almighty Beard-ed One." He chugged again.

I smiled. "You're right. I do believe in God. I believe Jesus to be His son. I believe He is as real as the beer in your hand. The jury is still out on the beard thing, though."

"For me, the jury is out on all of it – God, beard and all."

"So, you don't believe in God?"

"I don't think so," he replied.

"Not even a little bit?" I asked.

Julian dipped one of the bread sticks in the cheese dip. "I'm pretty sure I don't. Not even a little bit."

"How come?"

His eyebrows came together. "Because there is little evidence to suggest God exists. God started off as wishful thinking. Then He turned into a way for people to explain things they couldn't at the time – weather, plagues, astrology. But now we're finding logical and scientific explanations for everything. And we're evolving beyond creating a false sense of comfort."

"Many claim the evidence argument is quite the opposite: there is plenty of it. Those who don't see it *choose* not to see it. But suppose you're right. Suppose there is no evidence to support the existence of God. Why, then, do so many people still believe?" I asked.

"Don't take it too personally, but I think most people who believe in God are just a little less intelligent than those of us who know better. They haven't caught up to those of us ahead in the pack. Once the cat is out of the bag, popular opinion will flip. Think about it. We have record of existence for, perhaps, 6,000 thousand years. And just in the last century alone have people begun to be allowed to question the existence of God without being burned alive or exiled. Give it some time. Things will turn."

"Look, Julian. Don't worry about offending me. I've heard this before. I've considered it myself. I definitely see the appeal. I respect your sincerity. I respect your sincerity with yourself. Whether or not you believe in God doesn't change the fact that I think you're a great guy," I told him.

Respecting Julian did not mean I didn't have a burden for his soul. Over the next year and a half, Julian and I had many more conversations. They included every topic under the sun: family, history, literature, philosophy and yes, God. Or, as he often liked to correct me, "the absence of God." We even swapped books. He gave me Bertrand Russell's *Why I Am Not a Christian* and George Smith's *Atheism: The Case Against God*. And I gave him John Stott's *Basic Christianity* and C.S. Lewis'

Mere Christianity. We discussed the books. I told him why I disagreed with Mr. Russell and Smith and he told me why he couldn't swallow Lewis' testimony.

I was starting to wonder if Julian would ever come around. I'd spent so much time with him. I'd grown to really love the guy. It pained me to think that the man would not spend eternity in Heaven. I wanted to see him there.

One day I told him, "Julian, I think you want God to be real."

He thought for a second as his eyeballs rolled back. To my surprise, he said, "Maybe that's true. The idea of God is comforting, for the most part anyway." He looked amused.

"Why else would your mind be so preoccupied with God? Why would you spend so much time with someone who believes in God? I think you're hoping I can convince you He exists," I said.

He pursed his lips. "Although I don't agree, I could see how you might think that."

"I also think that you *don't* want to believe," I added.

"Why would I wish God exists, yet fight the urge to believe at the same time?"

"I don't know. You're the one doing it."

We went back and forth for a bit. Finally, he said, "Okay, Mark. Maybe I *do* want to believe. But I can't. I just can't. It seems so stupid. So illogical!"

"If you want to believe, are you willing to do what I tell you?" I asked.

"Sure…?"

"What are you afraid of…since God doesn't exist?"

"Nothing. It's fine. I'll do it. What is it?"

"I want you to say this prayer."

"But I don't believe in God."

"Hey, you said you'll do what I tell you!"

He chuckled and threw his head back. "Alright, alright. Let's hear it."

"God, I don't believe you exist. *But* if you do exist, show me and cause me to understand that this is You. And if You show me I will believe, not just in You, but that You are the Father, that Jesus Christ is your son, the Savior and then I will repent of my sins. I will turn away from my old self, and give my life to Christ. And I'll follow You the rest of my life."

He looked up.

"Julian, are you willing to say that…since you don't believe?"

"Sure."

In the dramatic fashion that had somehow become routine, I was awakened by violent knocking one Saturday morning at one o'clock. At first I thought it was a dream. When Christine had reassured me it was real knocking on our apartment door, and insisted it was the man's job to check it out, I began scrolling through a list of people I might have offended and pushed them over the edge and to the other side of my entrance door. Fortunately, the knocker identified himself before I gave my wife reason to question my manhood. "Mark, it's me, Julian! I need to talk to you!" Then he knocked again.

"I'm coming," I hollered back. I put the broom back in its place and unlocked the front door.

Julian's hands were trembling, his eyes open wide, sweat was pouring down his forehead and his hair was frazzled like a mad scientist's.

"Julian, what's going on? Is everything alright with the family?" I asked.

"Everyone is fine." He frantically stepped inside and I closed the door. Christine came in to see the man responsible for the commotion.

"I got it," I told her.

"Mark, I prayed the prayer."

"What prayer?" I hadn't talked to Julian in weeks.

"The one—"

"Oh, yeah." I rubbed my eyes. "Sit down." I pointed to the kitchen chairs.

"You were saying…"

"I prayed the prayer exactly like you said."

"Okay…"

"And then I was electrocuted."

It was late. I thought Julian just told me he was electrocuted. "Say that again? What happened?"

"I was electrocuted."

I tapped the table with my fingers. I blinked a few quick flashes. "What do you mean?"

"Have you ever been electrocuted by anything?" Julian asked.

"Yeah, sure – batteries, televisions, electrical outlets."

"When I said the prayer, I felt, not a small shock, but" – he raised his arm above his head and then dropped it forcefully, "I felt something like a big bolt of lightning. It went from the top of my head all the way down to my toes. I thought my body was being split into thousands of particles. I thought I was dying. I was sure of it. I was rattled like a salt shaker."

"Wow, Julian." I stopped tapping the table.

"Julian, I have to say." I shook my head. "God must love you in a special way…because He never showed me that kind of proof…or anybody else that I know. You know what this is?"

"What?"

"This is a very special revelation very few people have," I said.

For the next minute no one said anything.

"So, what's next?" I asked.

"I need to follow through on what I said," he said.

I invited Julian to allow me to lead him in prayer. We moved and knelt on the floor of the living room. I led Julian in prayer. He asked to be forgiven of his sins, and surrendered his life to Jesus.

- - -

When I was looking to get to freedom, I didn't know what exactly I hungered for. Not that political freedom isn't to be sought after or cherished. Because it is, and I value it greatly. But there is a freedom that surpasses political freedom. It is the eternal freedom that Christ offers. It is firm and everlasting.

The world is full of people looking for everlasting freedom. No doubt, you know at least one such person. It is the job of those of us who've already crossed over the fence to show those who don't have the map the right way to go.

Be on mission where you live, work and play. You never know when lightning will strike.

ACKNOWLEDGMENTS:

MARK:

This story would not exist and I would not be the same without the following people.

My maternal grand-grandfather, Taica Radu, who introduced Biblical faith to our family. And thank you Lord for putting a man with a Bible next to Taica Radu in the trenches of war.

My paternal grandfather Taica Ion not only impacted me with his love and kindness, but he planted the seed of the idea of living in the West.

I'm grateful that Bunicu Iosif Adler and Bunica Ana Adler risked their lives to immigrate to Australia after World War II and would one day have an amazing granddaughter in Christine, who would be waiting for me just as I hit Australian soil.

Mom and Dad demonstrated selfless love and showed my sisters and I what it means to serve God and to love other people. There aren't enough words to justify my indebtedness to them.

My sisters Petra (Pepi), Mary, and Chivuta (Vickie) took care of their little brother and provided enough childhood memories to last a lifetime.

Fratele Toma Toma sought me out and invited me to a gathering of believers hours after my landing in a new world. Who knows where I might be without his obedience.

I would definitely not be the person I am today without my parents-in-law, Peter and Anna Velja. Only eternity will reveal the impact of the love and time they invested in me has had.

My partners and co-pursuers of freedom, wherever they may be now: Genu, Nick, Lucian, and Johnny. Am I glad I got mixed up with those crazy guys. Your friendship and support, especially during our defection, was priceless.

PAUL:

There is a vast open field of gratitude I owe to so many.

Mark trusted me with his story. He envisioned this project, and my being an integral part of it, before uttering a word. Thank you, Mark. Thank you Ovi Cioloca, Emi Izvoranu, Nathan Kloes, Peter Kendric, Noemi Kalath, and Ian Hurlburt for taking the time to read the entire manuscript in its infant stages and giving us invaluable feedback. We are blessed to know you all. Paul Bara and Raz Pataca provided their design and technical expertise and built us a cyber platform to tell the world about this project – thanks for bearing with us.

Thanks you Mark Snowden for cleaning up our story so we could shop it. A bottomless pit of appreciation goes out to the wonderful Anna McHargue and the creative and patient sales and marketing team at Elevate for the sweat you put into this project. We didn't always make things easy. Much appreciation goes to Robby Lutrell for providing the initial spark for this project. Keep that reel rollin', Robby. Mark Russell took a chance on us, and I can't say enough about that.

Most of all, I'm grateful to God for not only blessing me with a love for story and words, but for revealing that love and putting so many amazing people in my life.

ABOUT THE AUTHORS

Mark Hobafcovich is a Christian leader and author. He studied at Victoria Bible College in Melbourne, Australia and Baptist Theological College of Queensland in Brisbane, Australia. Since 1982 has served as pastor church-planter in Australia and the United States where, since 1997 has served with the Southern Baptist Convention's North American Mission Board mobilizing pastors and churches to impact the world with the good news of the gospel. Mark believes that making disciples of all people (Matthew 28:16-20) is not only the Lord Jesus Christ's commandment but also every believer's privilege as His followers, and it ought to be our first priority. He lives in metro Atlanta with his wife, Christine.

Paul Dragu is a freelance writer who was instructed under novelist Tom Hyman. His work has been featured in the magazine, *Thoughts About God,* and the travel guide, *EscapeWizard.com.* In addition, Paul has also contributed to *RedState* and *Patch.com.* He also lives in Atlanta, Georgia.

elevate publishing

A strategic publisher empowering authors to strengthen their brand.

Visit Elevate Publishing for our latest offerings.
www.elevatepub.com

NO TREES WERE HARMED IN THE MAKING OF THIS BOOK

OK, so a few
did need to make the ultimate sacrifice.

In order to steward our environment,
we are partnering with *Plant With Purpose*, to plant
a tree for every tree that paid the price for the printing of
this book.

⟶ PLANT WITH PURPOSE

www.plantwithpurpose.org

go to www.elevatepub.com/about to learn more